GW01377074

The Jews
of Devon and Cornwall

Essays and Exhibition Catalogue

The Hidden Legacy Foundation

First published for The Hidden Legacy Foundation in 2000
by Redcliffe Press Ltd, 81g Pembroke Road, Bristol BS8 3EA

Text © the authors

ISBN 1 900178 82 6

British Library Cataloguing in Publication Data
A catalogue record for this book is available from The British Library

All rights reserved. No part of this publication may be reproduced, stored in a retrieval system, or transmitted, in any form or by any means, electronic, mechanical, photocopying, recording or otherwise, without the prior consent of the publishers.

Typeset by Mayhew Typesetting, Rhayader, Powys
and printed by WBC Print, Bridgend, Mid Glamorgan

Contents

Introduction *Evelyn Friedlander*	5
Judaism and the Jewish People *Albert Friedlander*	7
Synagogues and Cemeteries in the South-West *Helen Fry/Evelyn Friedlander*	12
The Rabbis and Ministers *Frank Gent*	26
Nathan Joseph Altmann *Bernard Susser/ ed. Evelyn Friedlander*	32
Lemon Hart *Evelyn Friedlander*	37
Solomon Alexander Hart RA 1806–1881 *Julia Weiner*	41
Ezekiel Abraham Ezekiel of Exeter *Frank Gent*	51
The Jews of Barnstaple *Helen Fry*	61
Exhibition Dates	65
Lenders	66
The Catalogue	67
Glossary	117
Selected Bibliography	119
Contributors	120
Acknowledgements	121
Photo-Credits	122

Exhibition/catalogue credits

Exhibition

The Hidden Legacy Foundation

Designers

Fritz Armbruster
Rupert Gebhard

Curators

Evelyn Friedlander
Helen Fry

Assistant Curator

Frank Gent

Photographic Curator

Frank Dabba Smith

Exhibition Concept

Evelyn Friedlander
Helen Fry
Eva Grabherr
Frank Dabba Smith

Catalogue

Evelyn Friedlander, editor
Fritz Armbruster, cover design

Introduction

EVELYN FRIEDLANDER

The idea for the exhibition was sparked off by visits to the Plymouth Hebrew Congregation and the Exeter Hebrew Congregation and seeing their magnificent collections of ritual silver. First, it was all catalogued by Dr. Annette Weber of the Frankfurt Jewish Museum. Then, intrigued by the notion of communities who had both the money and the taste to acquire such beautiful objects, I decided to find out more about them.

I had been introduced to the South-West of England by Dr. Helen Fry, who at that time lived in Exeter. She took me to the various Jewish cemeteries and synagogues and introduced me to her many friends there, who have contributed in no small measure to this exhibition.

Usually, when developing the concept of an exhibition, one has a theme and then sets out to find the objects to illustrate it. This was not the case here. As extraordinary as the collections of silver are, this was never intended to be an exhibition about Anglo-Jewish silver (which may come at a later date). We had to scour museums and archives to see what else might still be extant. Once all the available material had been located, what emerged from the artefacts were the stories of four communities and of some of the people who had lived and flourished in them over a span of some two hundred years. We have concentrated on the origins of the synagogue and the meaning and role of the Torah in Jewish life, and continued with important personalities from the region, many of whom had an impact well beyond their home counties. We have deliberately not dealt with either the Jewish life cycle or the Festivals. Suitable artefacts were not available and, in any case, this information can be gleaned from textbooks.

Having several short essays alongside the catalogue offered the opportunity to add material which would deepen and add specialist background knowledge, since there was much that could not be tackled in the exhibition itself. Thus there is an occasional and inevitable overlap or repetition of information.

For Helen Fry, my co-curator and myself, our fervent wish is that the exhibition communicates something of the atmosphere of this world; to this end, there are a number of people to whom we would like to record our thanks. First of all, our

INTRODUCTION

greatest thanks go to Fritz Armbruster, the designer of the exhibition, without whom it would not have been possible; his help, support and enthusiasm were invaluable. Frank Dabba Smith has been responsible for dealing with all aspects of the photography and Frank Gent joined the team at a late stage, and made an enormous contribution. At an early stage, Eva Grabherr shared her experience in setting up exhibitions and to all of them go our profound thanks for their scholarship, their expertise and for the sheer pleasure of working with them.

Initial research for this project was funded by The Hidden Legacy Foundation, while further funding for the exhibition has come from the Rothschild Foundation, the Littman Foundation, Lady Hoare, the Steele Charitable Trust, the Ann and David Susman Charitable Trust, Caroline Roboh, the Spalding Foundation, the Ralph Collett Will Trust, the Sieff Charitable Trust, Lady Grade, the Worshipful Company of Weavers, the David Syme Memorial Fund, the Rayne Foundation, the Elizabeth and Sidney Corob Foundation, the Maurice Wohl Charitable Trust, the Ralph and Muriel Emanuel Charitable Trust, Anton Felton, Lady Lever, and the Matthew Hodder Charitable Trust. To all of them go our heartfelt thanks.

As ever for the Hidden Legacy Foundation, there has been a far-flung national and international co-operation in evidence here, and once again it has been a complicated way of working. We hope the rewards are justified in the pleasure and knowledge which visitors to the exhibition will surely enjoy.

Evelyn Friedlander
Director of The Hidden Legacy Foundation

Judaism and the Jewish People

ALBERT H. FRIEDLANDER

There can be no Judaism without Jews. Libraries record vanished religions of ancient times, but Jews and their religion are found in communities throughout the world. At the beginning of this century, a Japanese emperor met a Jew. "What? You really exist?" he asked. "I thought Jews disappeared after the Bible was written." Others have thought so – or wanted to think so. In Christianity's early history, a Christian scholar tried to discard the Hebrew Bible together with the Jewish background of Christianity. He wanted his religion to be totally pure and unique. Today, Christian scholars know that they must study Judaism in order to understand how Christianity developed. They have also accepted that Jews and Judaism have existed for over 2000 years, and have much to teach the world.

The Hebrew Scriptures, usually referred to as 'The Old Testament' by Christians, is the record of Jewish life and religion from its very beginnings. When Babylon and later Rome conquered Israel, Jews were forced to live in the 'Diaspora', that is, outside the land of Israel. In time, Jewish communities were established in all the continents of the world, each community with its own individual story. When we study the history of Jewish migrations around the world, whether for example in Germany, the United States, Russia, or Cornwall, we see a clear pattern of an unusual history.

The Jews arrived in a strange country, fleeing from persecution in the land of their birth. They found lands which were free and open and welcomed newcomers; a better life was possible for them, whether they had come as individuals, as a small family, or as a flock of refugees. They settled in a new and different land, where other languages had to be learned, new customs acquired. Nevertheless, the central core of their life remained the same. Their homes continued to be filled with the ancient Jewish traditions, and their belief in God remained to fill their homes with warmth and beauty. Much of Judaism and its ideals live within the home and not only in a sanctuary. The Sabbath, with its candles, its prayers over wine and bread, and the blessing of the children, gave the Jews comfort in an often difficult and alien new world.

As the communities grew and became established, more was needed. First, as historical studies have verified, a community needs to acquire land in order to establish its own cemetery. Actually, this follows a Biblical precedent. It mirrors the history of Abraham as he approaches the inhabitants of his new land: "I am a stranger and sojourner in your midst," he tells them. He is mourning the death of his wife Sarah, and must buy a burial place for her. Thus, he is established as a permanent resident in the land, and his family and community history begins there. (Genesis, Chapter 23)

Even after communities have vanished or moved away, historians can examine the stones in the cemeteries of these earlier Jewish communities to discover much about them. Later, as the community grew and became established, it would buy or build a synagogue building. This would help to weld them into a congregation, with a *chevra kaddisha* (burial society), a Ladies' Guild and perhaps, if they had sufficient means, with a rabbi and even a *cantor* to lead them in prayer. Almost everything they did was then centred around the sacred scroll, the *Torah*, which was placed in the Holy Ark.

The Jews knew that in their Bible they possessed a special 'homeland': the world in which they lived might change as they travelled; but the Hebrew Bible, particularly the Pentateuch, endured as the foundation of their life. The *Torah* was the heart of Jewish life and thought. "As Israel has preserved the *Torah*, so the *Torah* has preserved Israel" may summarise Judaism. These Five Books of Moses contain the laws, customs, and beliefs which have endured for over 3,000 years. It is the Revelation of the Covenant between God and Israel, the sacred text which is augmented by the other books of the Hebrew Bible – the Prophets and Writings which give a detailed account of Jewish history, and of the quest to fulfil the purpose for which humans have been placed into the world by the One God, who sets us ethical standards. The shortest definition of Judaism is 'ethical monotheism', the belief that the One and only God is worshipped through ethical actions. From the beginning, the faith of their Christian neighbours was also built upon the most important teachings from the *Torah*, the Ten Commandments, with their injunctions to love their neighbours, to show compassion to strangers, and all the ethical actions which Jesus taught them out of his Jewish tradition. Differences exist, but so, today, does the dialogue among religions.

Judaism was and is practised in the home as much as in the synagogue, and many ritual objects in the home serve as reminders to live a life as described in the *Torah*. The ceremonies have become part of the rich culture of Jewish life. There is a *mezuzah* attached to the lintel of the front door, as a reminder of the verse in the

Book of Deuteronomy (6.4–10), "and you shall place them upon the door posts of your homes". 'Them' here refers to the words of the central prayer of Judaism, the *Shema*, which states:

> Hear, O Israel, the Eternal our God, the Eternal is One and Unique. And you shall love the Eternal One, your God, with all your heart, and with all your soul, and with all your might. And these words, which I command you this day, shall be upon your heart; and you shall teach them diligently unto your children, and shall speak of them when you sit in your house, when you walk along the way, when you lie down, and when you rise up. And you shall bind them as a sign upon your hand, and they shall be for frontlets between your eyes. And you shall write them upon the doorposts of your house and upon your gates.

The text mentions other ritual objects which fill Jewish life: the *t'fillin*, leather phylacteries which are tied upon the arm and placed on the forehead as reminders of this prayer. And 'teaching the children' became so basic that not only in the home, but also in the synagogue and often in an adjoining school building, the children were instructed in the study of Hebrew so that they could be called up to the *bimah*, the pulpit, to read the *Torah* Scroll for their *bar mitzvah* (son of the commandment), in the difficult unpointed Hebrew, to show that they were ready to take part in the service itself. Today, Progressive Judaism instructs the girls as well for their *bat mitzvah* (daughter of the commandment).

In a very real sense, this service of 'accepting the Covenant' made the children full members of the community. The boy had already entered the Covenant on the eighth day of his life, through the *brit*, the Covenant Rite of Circumcision. One of the traditional customs of Jewish life in Ashkenazi synagogues in continental Europe, was to take the swaddling cloth of that rite, cut it into several strips which were then sewn together. It was then embroidered or painted with the date, the boy's name and that of his father, and finally decorated with words taken from a blessing – the wish that he might grow up to *Torah* and its study, to *chuppah*, a happy wedding, and to *Maasim Tovim*, to good deeds. That band then became a *mappa*, a binder placed around the *Torah*. The celebrations for these family events took place both in the synagogue and in the home, and the dietary laws in the *Torah* were always strictly observed.

After Biblical times, the *Talmud*, a later commentary and compendium of rabbinic laws to bring Biblical teachings into later times, specified the *kosher* laws. The forbidden food in the Bible included pork, shellfish and other seafood, and separated milk and meat dishes. Also, the rabbis devised special methods of ritual slaughter, which were enlightened for their time and sought to cause the animals minimum pain. Traditional communities, large or small, therefore needed the services of a *shochet*, a ritual slaughterer. Usually in small communities, the rabbi also had to act as both a *shochet* and a *mohel* (circumcisor), as there was no way that they could afford to hire more than one man. Often, particularly in the village communities of continental Europe, their neighbours catered to their needs: to this day, many bakers offer a special bread on Fridays (the braided *challah* which is part of the Sabbath evening home celebrations) without knowing how this custom arose. However, when it came to *mazzot*, the unleavened bread needed for Passover, the Jewish communities had to set up their own ovens.

When one turns to the synagogue itself, much of the above can be seen more clearly. Covering the Holy Ark, where the *Torah* Scrolls are kept, is the *parochet*, the curtain with various symbols representing Judaism. Often, we see the Ten Commandments written in Hebrew upon the Two Tablets of the Covenant; these tablets are sometimes supported by the Lions of Judah and surmounted by a crown, because the *Torah* is said to be the crown of Judaism. Other symbols might include a 'Tree of Life', a reminder that the *Torah* is seen as the basic support of life in a society where Jews have been persecuted. Nevertheless, Jews would not abandon their faith. They continued to trust in God, and did not turn away from the moral code and the teachings of hope, which made them believe that a better life was ultimately possible for all human beings.

What made such optimism possible for the Jews during all the centuries of persecution and darkness? There was, of course, the belief in the One God who cared for all humanity; and a strong faith that all humans possessed a spark of Divine goodness, even when they turned away from the righteous path and committed evil. *Rosh Ha-Shanah*, the Jewish New Year's Day, was a time of contemplation and repentance, as one examined one's life and behaviour throughout the previous year. It is a ten-day period of penitence, with *Yom Kippur*, the Day of Atonement, as the final, most solemn day of all. Even Jews who have become lax in their observances try to attend their traditional or progressive synagogues on that day. During those 25 hours of total fasting, one contemplates the wrongs that one may have done to others. One must attempt to undo these acts if possible, try to atone for them and show true repentance in order to win forgiveness. The very fact that there was a possibility of change and improvement made Judaism a more hopeful faith.

The calendar of Jewish festivals has been termed 'a catechism of Jewish beliefs' in its joyful celebration of freedom (Passover), the Feast of Weeks (*Shavuot*), which acknowledges Sinai and the Ten Commandments as a religious constitution for all the Children of Israel; and the various other feasts. They deal with the history of Israel but also emphasise the teachings of the Bible through which everyone must fulfil the God-given tasks which created the pathway through history from the time of Abraham until today. The children's role is acknowledged in all these celebrations, whether in the synagogue or in the home where the *Seder* home service for Passover permits them to ask questions and to assert themselves.

There are differences within the Jewish community – a vocal Progressive Judaism stands alongside the traditional bastion of Orthodoxy – but the community remains united in its basic beliefs. Its affirms God the Creator who has made a Covenant which Jews affirm freely in their lives. Both doubts and certainties are expressed in the prayer books of Jewish life. There is no catechism of dogmas to be memorised and affirmed; one is judged by righteous actions, and by the acceptance of individual and communal obligations. After the darkness of the Holocaust, Judaism still shows itself as a believing faith. The Biblical book of Job expresses the pain and the questions of undeserved suffering, but also the ultimate confidence in a God who cares for all of humanity, and who shares the pain of all his children. The twentieth century has shown the full capacity of evil which resides in human beings; but Jews also see the capacity for good, and the 'Righteous of the nations' who sometimes gave their lives to save Jews during the Holocaust are acknowledged in a Jerusalem institution (*Yad v'Shem*) where the names are collected and honoured. The great teachers of Judaism in the twentieth century, from Martin Buber to Leo Baeck, have explored the human dimensions and have discovered and re-affirmed that area of the encounter between the finite human being and infinite God. In that area, Judaism and Christianity, and the other ways that reach towards the Divine, find themselves as partners on the road of ethical action which leads towards the future.

Synagogues and Cemeteries in the South-West

HELEN FRY AND EVELYN FRIEDLANDER

The exhibition has focused primarily on the four historic Georgian synagogues and cemeteries of the South-West: Plymouth and Exeter, which still have places of worship, and Falmouth and Penzance which once had small but vibrant Jewish communities. However, in more recent times, there has been a functioning synagogue in use in Torquay as well as a cemetery situated in the neighbouring seaside town of Paignton. Mention will also be made of the 'Plymouth Dock Minyan', and the Truro cemetery, both of which are no longer in existence.

Plymouth Synagogue

A Jewish community had become sufficiently settled in Plymouth by the mid-eighteenth century that it warranted its own purpose-built synagogue and in 1759, it began planning to meet that objective. Prior to that, from about 1745, local Jews had held regular services in their own homes or in a rented room, as was then the pattern with many nascent communities. The Plymouth synagogue, eventually erected in 1762 and still used for services today, is the oldest Ashkenazi synagogue in Britain. It was built on land in Catherine Street with a lease granted on 27th April 1762 to "erect or build any houses or edifices thereon."[1] It was consecrated later that year.[2] The synagogue is quite visible from the road, although its entrance is to be found via a side alley. It has a simple yet elegant Georgian frontage. The foundation stone, inscribed in Hebrew, reads (in translation): "Holy to the Lord. This holy and honourable house was founded and built in the year, 'Come let us worship, bow down and bless before the Lord' (Psalms 95, 6 with slight changes; the year 5522 = 1761/1762)."

Opposite the entrance to the synagogue is another building known as Synagogue House, used as a home for the once-resident rabbi. It was completed by 1874, having moved from a site required by the corporation to build the Guildhall.[3] It also houses a disused *mikveh* dating from the nineteenth century, which can still be seen in the vestry, although it is in need of renovation.

Stained glass windows, Plymouth Synagogue. [photo: Helen Fry]

Silver *kiddush* cup, 1775, Plymouth synagogue. [photo: Frank Dabba Smith]

Visitors to the synagogue, perhaps familiar with the style of rural places of worship on the continent, may well be surprised at the similarities in the interior. 1762 was a peak period for such buildings in Europe, and since many of the community's founders originated from Alsace, the Rhineland or Bohemia, it was only natural that they should have brought their native style with them, and commissioned it in their new homeland.

The Ark faces east, as always, and is carved in a light wood in a neo-classic style with late Baroque flourishes and flanking columns. The upper panel, topped with a broken pediment, contains the Decalogue (the Ten Commandments) surmounted by two crowns, the usual symbol of the *Torah*. The *bimah* (reading desk) is centrally placed, facing eastwards towards the Ark, and made of a darker wood, matching the pews, which face inwards towards the centre of the synagogue.

The upper gallery for the women has a narrow ironwork grille, and is carried on slender, fluted columns, more decorative than functional, and the whole would have been lit by a large number of candles. There are numerous stained glass windows, which date mainly from the twentieth century, and memorialise various members of the community.

The community today possesses a unique collection of Anglo-Jewish ritual silver, such as a *kiddush* cup from 1775, which is still in regular use. However, for safety's sake the silver is deposited in a bank vault. There are also a number of textiles, which almost all date from the twentieth century. A notable exception is a *Torah* binder from 1802, a unique reminder of a custom which the immigrant Jews brought with them from their previous homeland, in this case Bohemia. Mention should, however, be made of a set of three matching textiles, "given by the important women of Plymouth" in 1923. A label sewn inside reads, "Specialists in *tallisim* (prayer shawls) & synagogue embroidery R. Mazin & Co. 144 Whitechapel Rd. London E.1." Meanwhile, much of the history and heritage of the Plymouth Jewish community remains largely undiscovered in archives yet to be fully researched and translated.

The Plymouth Cemeteries

The Plymouth community has two cemeteries: the oldest located in an historic part of the city on the Hoe,[4] and the second adjacent to the Old Cemetery near Central Park. Permission was granted for the first known Jewish burial in the city in 1744 in a private plot of land on the Hoe owned by a local Jewish woman, Sarah

Sherrenbeck.[5] Subsequent burials took place within this original garden, and there came a time when the area was insufficient to meet the community's burial needs. In 1758, three London Jewish merchants purchased land nearby, probably adjoining the Sherrenbeck garden. The cemetery was to be expanded a number of times.[6] Today a high wall flanks the burial ground so that the casual passer-by will not notice that in this quiet plot of land there are a number of Hebrew tombstones. The chapel, once used for the last burial and purification rites, no longer exists. The cemetery is now disused but maintained by the community, who battle valiantly with the ever-intrusive shrubs and undergrowth. Many of the tombstones are showing signs of weathering and have become illegible. Bernard Susser has written:

> After a careful study of the surviving tombstones in the old cemetery, I deciphered in all 146 inscriptions. It is highly likely that most of these will disappear in the course of the next half century. It is, therefore, a labour of love and gratitude to generations gone by to record at least those which were extant in the 1960s so that they may be available to future generations.[7]

The second cemetery was acquired in 1868 in Gifford Place, adjoining the Municipal Old Cemetery, near Central Park and is still used for burials today. It has an *ohel* (a small chapel), rebuilt in 1958, where prayers are recited and the last purification rites are performed.

Devonport (Plymouth Dock Minyan)

Although the main synagogue was in Catherine Street, it was not the only Jewish place of worship in Plymouth. There was another located in the docklands area of Plymouth, known as the Devonport community or 'The Plymouth Dock *Minyan*'. The community used a room in a building here, around, or just before, 1810 but by 1844 it had been discontinued.[8] A second '*Minyan* Room' was reputedly opened in 1907 at 66 Chapel Street,[9] although it was first mentioned only in *The Jewish Year Book* for 1914. This building was destroyed by bomb damage during the Blitz of 1941, as was so much of the city of Plymouth. No known description of the interiors of the two '*Minyan* Rooms' has come to light to convey any idea of their architecture or interior decor, although we do know that they were not purpose-built synagogues.

The relationship between the Plymouth community and Dock *Minyan* seems to have been amicable. On 10th July 1815, they held a joint meeting at which they drew up ten resolutions.[10] The fourth resolution stated that:

> The Dock place of Worship be open for the purpose of performing Divine Services every day throughout the year, save and except the days of the New Year and the Day of Atonement, when the members of the Dock Institution will cheerfully attend the *Shool* at Plymouth.

The Plymouth community loaned two *Sifrei Torah* for use by the Dock *Minyan* in worship, as attested to in the eighth resolution of 10th July 1815:

> That the Elders and Committee of Plymouth *Shool* be solicited for the loan of two *Sifrei Torah* (scrolls) with the [adornments] appended thereto belonging, and that an understanding be given to Plymouth *Shool* that in the event of the Dock Establishment ceasing to resolve the *Sifrei Torah* in question should again be returned to them in like manner they are received.

A pair of ritual objects from Devonport has survived and is now in the possession of the Plymouth Hebrew Congregation. The first is a silver filigree spice box, in the shape of a four-leaf clover. It was a gift from Mrs. B. Moss "of the Plymouth Dock", 21st June, 1778. The second inscription reads: "in consequence of the discontinuance thereof, presented to Plymouth *Shul*, Sept 1848." There is also a pair of *rimmonim* with the inscription: "these bells with *Torah* and pointer were presented to the Devonport Synagogue by Mrs E. Cohen, 13th Sept 1914." The Jewish Museum possesses a calendar, hand-written in a fine, cursive Hebrew script by Gittele, daughter of Baruch of Devonport (1831).

Eighteenth-century silver filigree spice box, Plymouth Dock *Minyan*. [photo: Frank Dabba Smith]

A few textiles are also extant, testifying to the existence of the former community; an Ark curtain in cream damask silk with a matching *Torah* mantle, was presented by Mr & Mrs Myer I. Roseman on 26th March 1915, and a further Ark curtain, cream with gold edging, was presented by Esther Bass "in memory of her husband who departed this life April 22nd, 1937."

Exeter Synagogue

Exeter Synagogue was built in 1763 and consecrated on 10th August 1764.[11] It can be found in an alley called Synagogue Place, off Mary Arches Street. It has a plain, white stucco exterior with one ground floor window to the right and three windows on the upper level. Two black pillars and a number of stone steps flank the main entrance. The exterior remains relatively unchanged from when it was first built, except that the upper floor had to be altered following bomb damage during the Second World War. Two pictures of the exterior and interior painted by John White in 1890 form part of an album of eleven pictures by various artists, which was commissioned by Sir Julian Goldsmid, Deputy Speaker of the House of Commons, and now in the Royal Albert Memorial Museum, Exeter.

Charles Samuels donated two photographs of the synagogue, dating from about 1915, to the same museum in 1933. The photograph of the exterior of the synagogue shows a mattress factory, which once existed opposite, in what was then one of the poorest parts of central Exeter. The end of Synagogue Place contained the entrance to overcrowded slum dwellings.[12] To the right of the synagogue, the photograph shows a building which housed both the *cheder* (religion school) and the minister until it was demolished in the 1960s. The photograph of the interior shows that it was then lit by gas lighting. The Ark has been repainted with black and gold columns and urns, and the gallery columns with stencil decoration in the style of Owen Jones.[13]

The synagogue has recently undergone extensive renovation and was rededicated at a special service on 11th July 1999.

The Exeter Cemeteries

Exeter has two Jewish cemeteries. The oldest burial ground is in Magdalen Road, and has limited space for future burials. From the road, one can look down into this picturesque walled cemetery, carefully tended by the local Jewish community. Its stones are primarily engraved in Hebrew lettering, with occasional English, most still legible, although inevitably some have weathered with time and can no longer be deciphered. The cemetery has seen over one hundred burials since the land was leased to the community in 1757, and since 1977 the community has owned the burial ground. The earliest stone to have survived is only partly legible and dates from 1807. None of the earliest headstones from the eighteenth century has survived. With their disappearance and the continuing decay of existing tombstones, their inscriptions and biographical details will be lost, unless they are catalogued and transcribed. They are another example of Anglo-Jewry's fast disappearing and often unrecorded heritage. The second burial ground is located in the Exwick area of Exeter and can cater for the foreseeable burial needs of the community.

Torquay Synagogue

The story of the Torquay and Paignton Hebrew Congregation is one of much more recent history. It was founded during the Second World War, primarily by evacuees from London,[14] when some 50 families were evacuated from London's Stamford Hill to Torbay in 1939–1940. Services were held in a church hall, which was rented on a permanent basis near the town centre. Prior to that, worship took place in a local *kosher* hotel, the Sandringham. During the war years, the community had a resident rabbi, but after the war, the families returned to Stamford Hill taking their rabbi with them.

In about 1950, when the church hall was no longer available, the remaining community used the first floor of a clothing factory in Abbey Road, owned by a local Jewish businessman, Mr Michael Laderman. The building no longer exists and is now the site of a block of flats. In the mid-1950s, the community moved their premises for a third time to the Old Town Hall, and was served by a full-time minister, Revd. Weiwow, from circa 1948–1978. The synagogue was licensed for marriages, and a copy of the synagogue marriage register can be found in the National Register Office. Minute books and other community records have been lost over the years and therefore much of the history may be hard to record for posterity.

Today the synagogue still exists on the upper floor of the Old Town Hall in Abbey Road. It is a plain, unassuming room containing the bare necessities for a service, an Ark, a reading desk, and several seats. Above the Ark, is a stone Decalogue, and to its right a *menorah*. The community possesses two *Torah* scrolls, purchased at the beginning of its existence. Each scroll has a mantle, one donated by

Mr Laderman, the other by Lily Cohen. There are two silver *yadim* (pointers), but with no inscriptions. The blue velvet cover on the reading desks reads: "Presented to the Torquay and Paignton Hebrew Congregation by Lily and Beatrice Cohen in memory of their dear parents Barnet and Sarah Cohen, March 1961".

A *Torah* mantle from Torquay is now in the possession of the Plymouth Hebrew Congregation. It is made of red velvet, embroidered with bright yellow lions, a crown and a Star of David. Along the bottom are the words in Hebrew: "This was given in honour of Feyge Leah Geffen to the Torquay Synagogue".

Sixty years on, a community that at its peak had 180 members can no longer make up a *minyan*, the minimum quorum of ten adult men required for a service, and its future now looks exceedingly bleak.

Synagogue: Old Town Hall, Torquay. [photo: Helen Fry]

Torquay & Paignton Hebrew Congregation Cemetery

In 1962, the Jews living in and around the Torquay area acquired their own land for use as a burial ground in Colley End Road, Paignton, rather than use the existing burial grounds in Exeter or Plymouth. The cemetery has its own chapel and a plaque reads:

> This tablet was presented by the Torquay and Paignton *Chevra Kaddisha* in memory of Sydney Solomon, President for many years, a founder and an honorary life president, in grateful recognition of devoted and valuable services rendered.

One unusual gravestone, lying just outside the Jewish burial area, is incised with both a Star of David and a cross, suggesting that one of the married couple interred here was Jewish, while the other was not. Since the 1960s, approximately 50 burials have taken place here.

A Hebrew/Christian gravestone in The Torquay & Paignton cemetery. [photo: Evelyn Friedlander]

Falmouth Synagogue

By 1766, there were enough Jewish families living in Falmouth to warrant the establishment of a synagogue, and as the community continued to grow, a second synagogue with a seating capacity of 80 was built on Smithick Hill in 1806, overlooking the harbour. It was said that this was so that the merchants could keep an eye on the packet boats entering and leaving the bay.

The original building still exists, outwardly largely unaltered, although nothing remains of the interior archi-

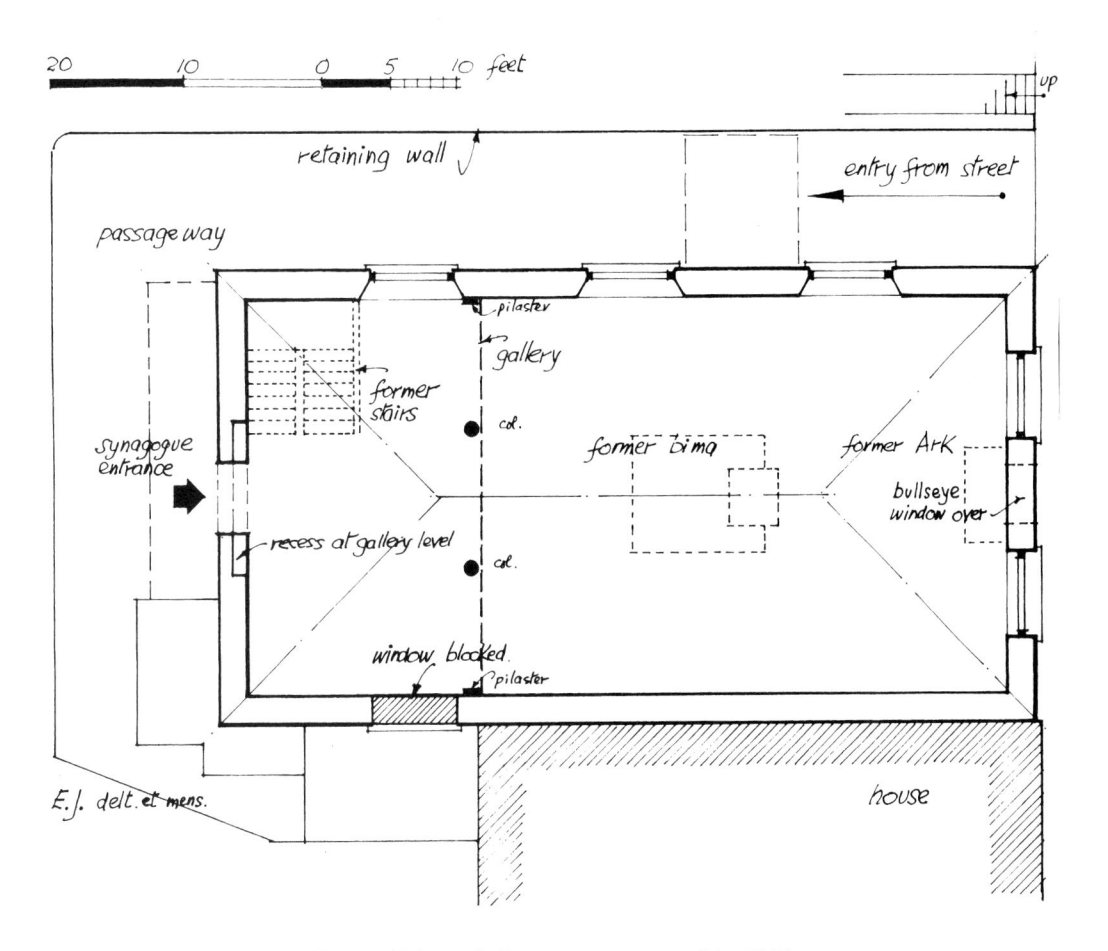

Former Falmouth Synagogue, surveyed in 1958.

tecture, except for one slender column, which would have supported the Ladies' Gallery, situated at the back of the synagogue on the west wall opposite the Ark. Its style has much in common with nineteenth-century non-Conformist chapels of the period, and its prominent location indicates the self-confidence of the Jewish community at that time. A survey made by Edward Jamilly[15] in 1958, when the building was in use as a furniture depository, shows the original main access at the rear, so that one would have entered from the street and walked around the building. The frontage faces east, where the ark would have been, and the central bulls-eye window over it was also a typical feature of German synagogues of this period. The doorway in the east wall was apparently added when the building became a cinema in a later incarnation. However, by 1881 the community had dwindled to such an extent as people moved to other parts of the country, that the synagogue was closed, and in 1892, the Chief Rabbi ordered its sale.

The last representative, Samuel Jacob, left for London in 1881, having first ensured that the synagogue was in good repair and after his death, his widow deposited the *Torah* scrolls for safekeeping in the Royal Institution of Cornwall in Truro. A pair of *rimmonim* and two pointers now in the Jewish Museum in London are all that is left of the ritual silver, along with the Decalogue that once surmounted the Ark.

Falmouth Cemetery

The Jewish cemetery lies several miles outside the town of Falmouth at Ponsharden, near Penryn. It is located on land that once belonged to the Bassett Estate of Tehidy, near Redruth. Lord de Dunstanville eventually gave it to the community.[16] The cemetery has seen over 50 burials, although a number of the gravestones are no longer visible. The weather and natural elements have again taken their toll and damaged the remaining headstones so badly that many of them are illegible. Fortunately, many stones had already been recorded, as a number of surveys have been carried out in the last hundred years.[17] The last burial was that of Nathan Vos in October 1913.

Penzance Synagogue

Part of the former Penzance synagogue, built in 1807-8, can still be seen by the visitor today, although it has now been almost entirely subsumed into the Star Inn on what is now known as Market Jew Street. The first purpose-built synagogue for the community had been built in 1768 in New Street, on the same site as the second one, on land leased from the Branwell family. Well hidden and tucked away in the heart of Penzance town centre, it was a rectangular building hung with slate tiles under a hipped roof and with brick walls. The east wall, which is all that is outwardly visible today, has two remaining arched windows, now boarded up and in urgent need of repair. Edward Jamilly also surveyed this building in 1958 and his drawing shows a central *bima* with a chandelier over, a railed Ark, bench seating for the men on two sides, with a Ladies' Gallery on the north and south walls.

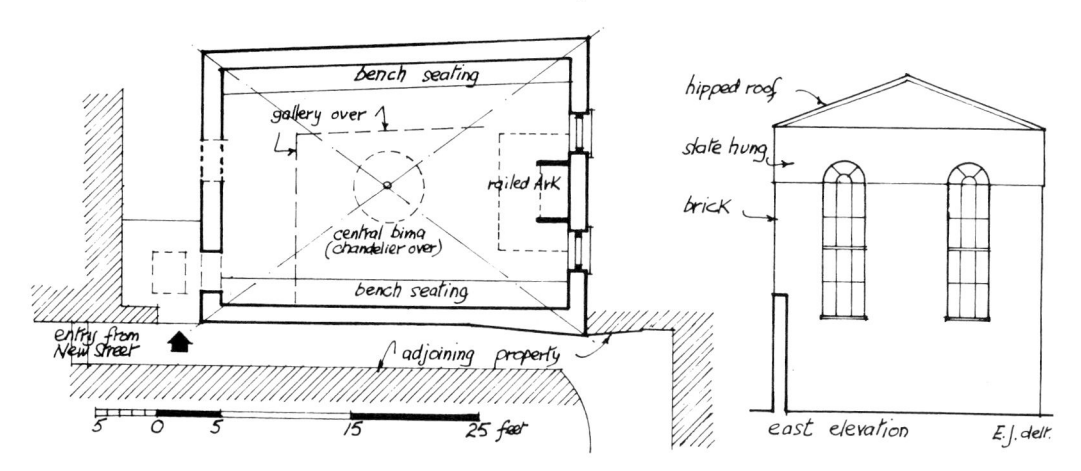

Former Penzance Synagogue, surveyed in 1958.

Two snapshots have recently come to light, the only other evidence of what the interior might have looked like. Taken around 1960, they date from a period when the building served as a church for the Plymouth Brethren. They do however show part of the Ark and the balustrades of the Ladies' Gallery. Apart from the Decalogue, which is now in the Jewish Museum, and in such poor condition that it could no longer be repaired, only a panel with a Hebrew inscription has survived. Not a single artefact could be traced, although we know from the minute books that there was once an extensive collection of *Torah* scrolls, silver ritual objects and textiles.[18]

Penzance Cemetery

The Penzance Jewish cemetery, acquired by lease around 1740, is located on a piece of land at the rear of Leskinnick Terrace, and its glorious location overlooking St. Michael's Mount Bay must make it one of the most beautiful cemeteries in the country. The recent deciphering of a tombstone fragment dates one of the earliest burials to 1741.[19] Until this discovery, it had been thought that the earliest burial had been in 1791.[20] The cemetery has 49 identifiable headstones, many in remarkably good condition.[21] Among the most striking is that of Jacob James Hart, Lemon Hart's nephew, who was appointed consul to the Kingdom of Saxony. Here lie buried B.A. Simmons and Isaac Bischofswerder, who both ministered to the Penzance community, members of the Oppenheim family, who owned a large store in the High Street, and the Bischofswerder, Jacob and Joseph families. All these families have descendants who are today scattered around the world. The last burial was that of Adolf Salzmann who died in 1964,[22] although a re-interment is scheduled to take place in the summer of 2000.

Truro Cemetery

Until recently, it was thought that the only two cemeteries which had existed for the Cornish Jewish communities were those in Falmouth and Penzance. New research has highlighted the existence of a Jewish cemetery in Truro dating from the late eighteenth or early nineteenth century.[23] It ceased to be in use by the mid-nineteenth century. Today, there are no visible remains, nor have any inscriptions from the tombstones been transcribed or listed. As with so much else, that part of the Anglo-Jewish heritage may well be lost to us.

NOTES

1. Formerly described as St Katherine's Lane. cf. Bernard Susser, *The Jews of South-West England*, The University of Exeter Press, 1993, p. 130.
2. For further details of the leases and conveyancing see Doris Black, *The Plymouth Synagogue 1761–1961*, 1961, pp. 17–18.
3. ibid. p. 19.
4. For a history of the cemetery and a transcription of the tombstones see Bernard Susser, *Tombstone Inscriptions in the Old Jewish Cemetery on the Hoe*, privately published, 1996 edition. For details of the cemetery leases, see also Black, 1961, p. 18.
5. cf. Susser, op. cit. pp. 126–8.
6. Black, 1961, p. 18. op. cit. See also Bernard Susser, 'Jewish Cemeteries in the West of England', in *Building Jerusalem*, ed. Sharman Kadish, Vallentine Mitchell, 1996, p. 158.
7. Susser, *Tombstones*, op. cit., p. 9.
8. Susser, *The Jews of South-West England*, op. cit. p. 130.
9. Susser, ibid.

[10] Printed in full in Black, op. cit. pp. 10–11.
[11] Date taken from an inscription in a Bible. cf. Susser. op. cit. and the website: http://www.eclipse.co.uk./exeshul/opening.htm.
[12] Information taken from the Exeter Synagogue website.
[13] ibid.
[14] We are grateful to Mr. Freed of the Torquay & Paignton Hebrew Congregation for providing details of the community's history.
[15] Our grateful thanks to Edward Jamilly for sharing this information with the authors.
[16] For a fuller history, see Keith Pearce and Godfrey Simmons, 'The Jewish Cemeteries', in *The Lost Jews of Cornwall*, ed. Keith Pearce and Helen Fry, Redcliffe Press, 2000, pp. 101–105.
[17] The findings of the different surveys have been published with new material in Keith Pearce and Godfrey Simmons, 'The Jewish Cemeteries', pp. 108–129.
[18] For a more detailed description, see Evelyn Friedlander and Helen Fry, 'The Disappearing Heritage' in Pearce and Fry, *The Lost Jews of Cornwall*.
[19] cf. Pearce and Simmons, 'The Jewish Cemeteries', op. cit. p. 131.
[20] cf. Susser, *The Jews of South-West England*, op. cit. p. 129.
[21] A complete transcript of the headstone inscriptions can be found in Pearce and Fry, *The Lost Jews of Cornwall*, pp. 133–154.
[22] Keith Pearce and Godfrey Simmons suggest that he may have been a refugee who settled in Redruth.
[23] See Pearce and Simmons 'The Jewish Cemeteries', op. cit., pp. 155–156.

The Rabbis and Ministers

FRANK GENT

The Jewish communities of Plymouth, Exeter, Penzance and Falmouth always strove to appoint a person to lead services. In addition, they needed someone to circumcise their sons, to teach their children, to officiate at weddings and funerals and to provide meat that complied with the Jewish rules of *kashrut*. Sometimes there were separate officiants to provide these various services, but usually economics dictated that the same individual provided them all. Although the minister is often given the title of rabbi, technically speaking very few of the ministers in nineteenth-century England were, as they had not received *semichah*; in other words, they were not ordained. The full functions of a rabbi were reserved to the Chief Rabbi in London, who supervised the clergy. These were appointed, usually on his recommendation, to serve the congregations, and he was deferred to on religious matters, which in turn enhanced his own authority.

The South-West congregations were well-served by their ministers, but the salaries they could pay were extremely low. The power of the lay leaders of each community was very great, and this led on several occasions to tensions and even breakdowns in the relationship. Plymouth, Exeter and Penzance had long-serving ministers in their earliest days, but by the second half of the nineteenth century it became increasingly difficult to find and retain a minister, many staying for only a year or two. Many of the ministers in the South-West went on to serve other, larger congregations in Britain, Australia, South Africa and the United States.

The Jewish community of Plymouth was always the largest of the South-West congregations, and managed to have a full complement of religious staff for most of its history. It was able to employ a full-time minister, sometimes known as the Reader, until the departure of Rabbi Susser in 1981. It also employed a cantor to lead the services until 1959, and a *shochet* at least until the end of the nineteenth century. At the same time as being able to employ these important functionaries, the leaders and other members of the community would themselves frequently be considerable scholars. For example, Lazarus Solomon from Lublin, a scholar (the term used is *torani*), in Plymouth before 1802, led the prayers in Plymouth Synagogue on the Days of Awe for 25 years. As the lay officers were the employers

THE RABBIS AND MINISTERS

of the minister and other officials this understandably led at times to conflict. The advice of the *Talmud* was for a rabbi to follow an occupation. This financial independence of the community must have been envied by their successors in the West Country. A similar situation continues today, where many communities prefer to manage without the services of a rabbi.

The names of most of the ministers, cantors and *shochetim* at Plymouth have been recorded in the late Rabbi Dr B. Susser's book, *The Jews of South-West England*. Details of their lives and work are fragmentary, but occasional glimpses appear from tombstones, legal papers and the correspondence of the Chief Rabbi.

The Rev. Myer Stadthagen was cantor of the Plymouth community from 1829 till his death in 1862, a period when he was also the religious leader of the community, but without the authority of a minister. Perhaps this reflected his lowly status when the congregation in 1828 first employed him as *shochet*. Stadthagen lived with his family at 21 Queen Street, Plymouth, adjacent to the synagogue. He came as a single man from Bischofswerder in Prussia in 1828 at the age of 24. His wife, Arabella (usually known as Bella) was from a Cornish family, the Josephs of Redruth. Their children were Selina, Phoebe, Isaac, Sarah and Ellen, but Isaac died in infancy. On his tombstone is inscribed "My only son Isaac, whom I loved, son of Meir, Cantor here. . ." Selina married in 1855, and her sister Sarah in 1860. They married in Plymouth; their sister Ellen married in Birmingham in 1864, two years after her father's death. In his will he requested that "the circumcision boxes shall be kept in the family until one of my grandchildren shall be a *mohel* [circumcisor]." Clearly he performed this function as an additional part of his duties, but with religious commitment. The loss of his only son grieved him, and he placed his hopes in a future grandson. Without a son, he left instructions in his will for *kaddish* to be said in his memory.

In addition to his duties as leader of the services, Stadthagen, at the Chief Rabbi's behest, regularly visited Jewish prisoners at Dartmoor – by then the railway line to Princetown was in existence – but sadly he was sometimes opposed in this work by the congregation. He also visited the sick and officiated at weddings and funerals. He fell out from time to time with members of the congregation, as is indicated in a letter from the Chief Rabbi in 1855, requesting that he drop a civil action for libel against Aaron Levy so as to avoid disgrace to the community.

A letter survives from 1867, recorded in Wilfred Jessop's unpublished work, *A Coat of Many Colours*, from Abraham Joseph of Plymouth, formerly the *shammas* (caretaker and factotum) at Penzance, to Chief Rabbi Dr. Adler. Abraham Joseph saw himself as a guardian of orthodoxy and tradition, and in this guise asked Dr.

Adler "to prevent an act which would give grave offence to many who remember what Plymouth was [...] but which has all now vanished." It seems that one Samuel Ralph, an apostate of 50 years and a mason's labourer, who had been married once or twice in church, had become very ill. Abraham Joseph learned that their minister had visited him, in response to a request from Samuel Ralph's brother, who did not wish him to be buried in a Christian cemetery. Abraham Joseph implored the Chief Rabbi that if he were drawn into the affair he would at least not allow Ralph to be buried in the main ground of the Jewish cemetery, but apart. Samuel Ralph died on 17th March and was buried on a raised plot separated from the rest of the cemetery. Abraham Joseph succeeded in maintaining orthodoxy as he perceived it.

Eventually Stadthagen, in sheer frustration, offered his resignation, but his troubles were cut short by his death. His tombstone records: "Here lies a man who walked in uprightness and righteousness, he feared the Lord God all the days of his life. 32 years he was cantor here in the Holy Congregation of Plymouth. Meir ben Rabbi Isaac, he died on Monday, the 7th day of Passover, aged 58 years and was buried with great honour on the last day of the Passover, 5622. Myer Stadthagen died 21 Nissan 5622 [=21 April 1862] aged 58." His successor was Levy Rosenbaum, a native of Poland, who held office for 30 years.

At Exeter there were very similar experiences. The first minister was the Rev. Moses Horwitz Levy, who remained for a remarkable 44 years. He is described on his tombstone in Exeter as a cantor and native of Danzig. His record was unmatched by his successors, both for *shalom beit* (peacefulness) and tenure. The Rev. Michael Levy Green came to Exeter in 1839 at the age of 28 on the recommendation of the Chief Rabbi. He had a reputation for being hot-tempered, which did not augur well for an appointment at Exeter. He married in June 1841, but fell out with the officers of the congregation when he opened a clothes shop to supplement his small income. Rather than surrender the shop, he left the ministry and went to London to embark on a successful business career.

The Rev. Samuel Hoffnung, an immigrant, succeeded him in 1841. Having come from Poland in 1836, he had first taken up a post at Newcastle before coming to Exeter. His dispute with Alexander Alexander, the distinguished president of the congregation, caused considerable scandal. The minutes of the congregation record the acrimonious row, seemingly inflamed by Mr Hoffnung's whipping of Mr Alexander's 15-year old son. There was another confrontation with a Mr Marks, which led to a complaint from Mr. Alexander to the Chief Rabbi, who wrote to Hoffnung: "Alexander the *Parnas* [President] has written to me that you broke into

THE RABBIS AND MINISTERS

a terrible passion in Synagogue and said to Marks, 'May you not reach the end of your journey.' Is this true?"

Hoffnung resigned, but his troubles were not over, for the community refused to pay his salary, leaving him destitute and unable to leave for another post. The Chief Rabbi rebuked Exeter for this, writing to Alexander, "I cannot suppress stating that no respectable reader will go now to Exeter to be exposed to such insults." Interestingly, unlike the officers, the members of the congregation appreciated Mr Hoffnung's services, and gave him a silver salver with the following inscription:

> Presented by Mr Moses Lazarus on behalf of the principal members of the Exeter Hebrew Congregation and Friends, to the Rev. S. Hoffnung, previous to his leaving the City, as a token of regard and esteem for his piety and zealous discharge of his duties during the last thirteen years. June 26th 5613 (1853).

Hoffnung's family eventually amassed a considerable fortune, but to their shame, the officers responded in a newspaper advertisement with a public repudiation of the gift Mr Hoffnung's family paid for the restoration of Exeter Synagogue in 1905.

Mr Hoffnung's successor, Berthold Albu, had similar experiences, and remained for only one year. The Rev. Myer Mendlessohn, another native of Prussia, came to Exeter when he was 22 and stayed for 13 years, but the congregation's decline led to his departure for Bristol in 1867. His reputation was remarkable, hardly ever falling out with the officers of the congregation. Henceforth Exeter was served by ministers whose stay was short. Exeter had become the lowest rung on the ladder of employment.

The Falmouth community's records have unfortunately been lost, and Rabbi Susser traced only five ministers. The earliest recorded minister, known as Rabbi Saavil, is buried at Falmouth. His tombstone records him as "Samuel son of Samuel Levi. Died 1 Nissan 5574 (22 March 1814) aged 73 years."

The tombstone of his successor, known as Rabbi Mowsha, reads "Moses son of Hayyim, Reader here in Falmouth." He died on 14th September 1830, only three years after the death of his 17-year old son Isaiah. He appears to have been known in English as the Rev. Moses Hyman, but a claim that he was minister for 27 years would indicate that his ministry started in 1803. It is possible that there were two ministers for a while, especially if his predecessor was a sick man. Joseph Benedict Rintel ministered in Falmouth until 1849, to be succeeded by a Mr Lipman. The last known minister was Samuel Herman, described in the 1851 census as "Rabbi of the Hebrew Congregation". Born in Konin, Poland, he lived in Killigrew Street, Falmouth, with his wife, son and two daughters.

THE RABBIS AND MINISTERS

There are traces of other religious life in Falmouth, in the form of the periodic examination of the *shochet* by the Chief Rabbi. A Mr Rubinstein was thus examined in 1868, similarly Mr A. Abbelson in 1872. The Jewish community of Penzance was also able to employ religious officials throughout most of its history, and to count on the considerable religious knowledge and expertise of some of its members.

Undoubtedly the record of Barnett Simmons, minister at Penzance from 1811 to 1859, with two brief interruptions, is remarkable. He is described in the 1851 census as 'Jew Minister' aged 67, born in Middlesex. Although he held office for such a long period, his early days were difficult. Originally appointed as *shochet* in 1811, he was frequently in dispute with the congregation.

Simmons was succeeded by the Rev. Hyman Greenburgh. There is a tombstone at Penzance for Samuel Hillman, son of Simeon Greenberg, who died in 1861, aged 24, which indicates that he was only 20 years old when he came to Penzance.

After a minister who stayed for one year, and a *shochet* named Rittenberg who was examined by the Chief Rabbi in 1868, the Bischofswerder family came to Penzance in 1874 and made their mark. The Rev. Isaac Bischofswerder ministered to the community until 1886, acting as reader and *shochet*, and was buried in Penzance when he died on 18th October, 1899, aged 77.

The Penzance community is said to date from 1807, but in fact there was an earlier minister than those hitherto listed. In Israel Solomon's well-known *Records of my Family*, published in 1887, is the following account:

> Mr Phillip Samuel ... was a native of Warsaw, and his life was full of romance. He was the son of the secretary of the Great Synagogue there, and highly educated in Hebrew. Marriages in Poland in those days were arranged at an early age, and his marriage was not a happy one. He had one daughter, who married, but her name I have forgotten. ... He arrived at last in England; but the life of the ordinary Polish emigrant, supported by peddling, was disgusting to the educated Phillip. Visiting at the house of the Chief Rabbi, Herschell, the rabbi got him the place as reader of prayers in the synagogue at Penzance, in Cornwall.
>
> For this he was not fitted. Attached to this office was then the slaughtering of cattle and poultry kosher, and as about this time the trade of collecting gold for government requirements to pay troops and war supply in the Continental war with the first Napoleon was profitable, he became an agent for buying gold for my uncle, Lyon Joseph, of Falmouth. Phillip trusted some money to a fellow polander to purchase gold, and the poor fellow, who was named Valentine, was enticed by a landlord at Plymouth Dock, and murdered. The murderer was discovered and hanged.

This event can be dated from other evidence. Valentine's tombstone at Plymouth reads: "Joshua Falk son of the late Isaac from Breslau. He was slain in the place of Fowey by the uncircumcised and impure man Wyatt and drowned in the waters, 14 Kislev 5572 and buried on the 17th thereof (30th November, 1811), aged 26 years."

Phillip Samuel's experiences were typical of many of the ministers who served the South-West. As an educated man, he did not enjoy his lowly status as a servant of his community. The minister might pray, then as now, "I am the servant of the Holy one, blessed be he", but the oligarchic leaders of the communities often expected too much for very little reward.

Nathan Joseph Altmann

NOTES LEFT BY BERNARD SUSSER EDITED BY EVELYN FRIEDLANDER

Hebrew name: Nathan Nota ben Joseph K"Z, i.e. he and his sons were *cohenim*, that is, priests in the Jewish tradition.

He was born in 1766 and died on 12th October 1849, and was buried in Plymouth Hoe Cemetery.[1]

He married Brina, the daughter of Abraham Joseph (b. 1731 Germany, d. 1794 Plymouth). "He (Abraham Joseph) was one of the people called Jews, but the actions of his whole life would have done honour to any persuasion" (*The Gentleman's Magazine*, 1794, p. 1194). By warrant he was appointed slopman to HRH Prince William Henry (later William IV), the third son of George III, a royal patronage which continued for three generations. Brina was born in Plymouth in 1781, and died on 23rd August 1865 at 15 Queen Street, Plymouth. She too was buried in the cemetery on Plymouth Hoe.[2] The 1851 Census described her as an annuitant and proprietress of houses. In the 1861 Census she is described as a Gentlewoman.

Amongst the effects of the Plymouth Hebrew Congregation in the 1960s was a textile which has now disappeared. It seems to have been a cloth to cover the *Sefer Torah* during the Reading of the Law. Known now only through a photograph, it had embroidered upon it the priestly hands raised in blessing, unusually viewed from behind and covered in fine lace gloves, surmounted by the crown of Torah, with the following inscription:

Cloth to cover the *Sefer Torah*.

> This belongs to the honourable Nathan son of the late Joseph of blessed memory and his spouse Mistress Breinelah daughter of

the honourable the late Abraham Isaac of blessed memory in the year, 'and may He give you the blessing of Abraham' (Genesis 28; 4).[3]

It is not possible to say whether this cloth or the *mappa* (*Torah* binder) referred to below was embroidered by Brina herself. The textiles are not the work of the same hand, as one is vastly more elaborate than the other, and was probably embroidered by a professional.

"13th August 1801 – ... I forever renounce and disclaim of all the possessions of my father Joseph Altmann Inhabiter of the Herrshaft of Ronsperg in the town of Roneberg Co. Klattauer Kingdom of Bohemia, to which possessions being the first born son I might be intitled to, as well local as Familiae Numerum, and that I transfer them to my second brother Joachim Altmann who in consideration thereof is to be married to Miss Theresa Mosses. As I am now near 18 years in the Kingdom of England, in the town of Plymouth established and settled and having no children ... Nathan Joseph Altmann."[4]

But on 3rd December 1801 (JJC 39) Brina and Nathan's son Abraham was born. To mark the occasion of his birth, they presented the congregation with a *mappa* (a binder for the *Torah* Scroll), perhaps embroidered by her, which was used in the Plymouth Synagogue. It is noteworthy that this custom was brought from German-speaking lands to England,[5] even though the mother was English-born, and that this binder is one of the only English-made circumcision binders known in this country. The traditional inscription on it reads:

> Abraham ben Nathan Nota KZ born for good luck on Thursday 28 Kislev '562 [= 3rd December 1801]. May the Lord rear him to the *Torah*, to the *Chuppa*, and to good deeds. Amen. Selah.[6]

An A. Altman Joseph, presumably this same child, was a member of the Plymouth Congregation in 1819 and in 1832.[7]

Another son, Sampson, was born on 3rd January 1804 (JJC 42). Their third child, Julia, died at the home of her sister, Mrs G.J. Asher, in Montreal on 25th August 1878 (I have no reference for this). Simha ben Isaac HaLevi was probably the son-in-law (B of R Ib). A daughter Annie, b. 1823, married Jesse Lawrence 1862 (PMR 48).

According to the 1798-1803 Plymouth Aliens' Register, Nathan Joseph was born in 1766 in Ranspork, Bohemia, and landed at Gravesend in 1784. He was a jeweller in Dartmouth from 1784 until 1802, and in Broad Street, Plymouth from 1802. He was a member of the Plymouth Meshivat Nefesh [Friendly] Society from 1795 until at least 1825.

He was a member of the Plymouth Hebrew Congregation and in 1819 was paying five guineas per annum for his seat. He must have had a large household, which ate well, as his bill in that year was reduced by two guineas meat tax. The butcher paid over to the congregation one farthing for every pound weight of meat purchased by a customer, and this amount was credited to the customer's synagogue account. Two guineas amounted to 2,016 farthings, so the Joseph household in 1819 was consuming just under 40 lbs. of meat every week.[8]

On 10th August 1828 he moved to London. Between 1801 and 1805 he was the occupier-proprietor of a house in Great George Street, Plymouth, where he paid twelve shillings per annum rent in order to be attached to the water conduit system. In 1806 he was registered as paying eight shillings per week conduit rent.[9]

He was a Navy Agent in Frankfort Place,[10] and at 72 Fore Street, Devonport (the same address as his brother-in-law, Joseph Joseph) in 1816.[11]

In 1822 he described himself as a mercer and draper and advertised that he would remove on Ladyday from Lower Broad Street.[12] In 1823 he is listed as a linen and wool draper at 9 Higher Broad Street, Plymouth.[13] On 24th November 1815 he signed a lease for water in a house in Union Street, Plymouth, inhabited by a Mr Little.

In 1825 he was one of 116 prominent Plymouth businessmen who declared that they had confidence in the Plymouth Naval Bank.

His will[14] refers to him as Nathan Joseph of Plymouth, Navy Agent. It recites an indenture of 31st March 1814 (Phineas Johnson of the 1st part; Joseph Joseph and his wife Edal of the 2nd part; Rosey Joseph and the said Joseph Joseph of the 3rd part; Abraham Aaron and his wife Phoebe, Nathan Joseph and his wife Brimey (sic), Esther Joseph, Edmund Lockyer of the 4th part), by which the Joseph family had borrowed £3,350 from Phineas Johnson on the security of certain lands.

Phineas Johnson called on Joseph Joseph to repay the debt, and Abraham Aaron, at the request of Joseph Joseph, advanced £1,030 and Rosey Joseph and Joseph Joseph advanced the remainder out of trust monies (arising out of the will of Abraham Joseph, 22nd October 1794, by which he left his property to his wife Rosey Joseph, his sons Joseph Joseph and Samuel Joseph in trust for Rosey Joseph, and his daughters Phoebe Aaron, Brimey Joseph, Esther Joseph and their children).

Phineas Johnson then sold to Joseph Joseph two messuages in Friary Street, a parcel of ground in New Street together with warehouses built thereon by Joseph Joseph, a messuage in Great George Street then occupied by Hyman Hyman, a cellar in Castle Street by the Brunswick Inn (then called Barbican House), a messuage erected by Thomas Lockyer then called the Island House and now the

Fisherman's Steps on Southside Quay or Barbican, then tenanted by Frederick Ralph.

The will continues by saying that Rosey Joseph, Abraham Aaron and Esther Joseph were dead and that Joseph Joseph had been adjudged bankrupt after 1814 but prior to bankruptcy the debt (to Abraham Aaron's heirs and the Trust Fund) had been reduced to £2,550 with large arrears of interest. The debt now stood as follows:

Abraham Aaron's children in their own right	£558.12.0
Brimey Joseph my wife & as personal representative of Rosey Joseph, Esther Joseph,	£1,017.12.0
Mosely Moses Alman	£324.12.0
& Jane Moses	£324.12.0
& Joseph Joseph	£324.12.0

"Now I bequeath to my wife Briney, and my sons Sampson Altman of Kingston, Jamaica, Surgeon, and Michael Israel Altman Kingston, Jamaica, Surgeon, everything.

Dated 7 August 1845 [Signed in Hebrew] Nathan Nota ben Joseph HaCohen."

The will was witnessed by Alfred Rooker, Solicitor. Reverend Myer Stadthagen and Alfred Rooker appeared on 25th August 1851 to prove the will. Stadthagen declared that the Hebrew sign was the signature of Nathan Joseph and that Cohen "was his Hebrew title or distinction".

It is surely significant that after more than sixty years residence in England he signed his will in Hebrew with his Jewish name.

NOTES

[1] Bernard Susser, *Tombstone Inscriptions in the Old Jewish Cemetery on Plymouth Hoe*, privately published 1996. Tomb B15.
[2] ibid. Tomb B108, JC.
[3] The chronogram gives the year '575 = 1815 (see photo).
[4] Worth, Plymouth Records.

[5] For an explanation of this custom, see Annette Weber, Evelyn Friedlander and Fritz Armbruster editors, *Mappot . . . Blessed be who comes*, Osnabrück 1997.
[6] See Bernard Susser, *The Jews of South-West England*, Exeter, 1993 p. 184.
[7] Plymouth Vestry Book 159, 245.
[8] Plymouth Hebrew Congregation Vestry Book p. 159.
[9] Plymouth Town Rental Books.
[10] Plymouth Directory 1812.
[11] Navy List 1816.
[12] Tapp 1822.
[13] Plymouth Directory 1823.
[14] PCC 736, 1851.

Lemon Hart

EVELYN FRIEDLANDER

For someone whose name is still known to any connoisseur of rum, remarkably little has actually been written about the man who gave his name to Lemon Hart Rum.[1] The bare facts of his life are these. He was born in Penzance on 31st October 1768, the son of Lazarus (Eliezer) Hart and was originally called Asher. In the burial register of the Great Synagogue, 1837–1854, he is listed in Hebrew as *Parness* (Elder) Rav Lemmle bar Eliezer, whereas in the Brady Street Cemetery register, he is listed as Parness Rav Asher bar Eliezer. In both cases, his English appellation is Lemon Hart. Tradition has it that the Hart family came from Weinheim in Germany.

In the course of the eighteenth century, rum trading really came into its own. In the year 1720, Abraham Hart settled in Penzance, and like so many people living in the West Country, he is said to have traded in sugar and rum with the West Indies. By the time he died in 1784, his son, Lazarus, was profitably engaged in trade. In 1777,[2] he had listed himself as a silversmith and slop (ready-made clothes) seller, in 1785 as a silversmith, shopkeeper and pawnbroker, and by 1799 as a merchant, a reflection of his growing status. Abraham's grandson, Lemon Hart, eventually took over his grandfather's wine and spirit business, which was to become renowned, and one of whose principal activities may have been the supplying of rum to the Royal Navy.[3] It was possible that he imported the rum and supplied it to Navy agents. One cannot be more specific, as so much of the company's history has come down to us in mythic form with no extant documentation.

Having moved to London in the first decade of the nineteenth century, he set up a partnership there, together with his brother, subscribing the total capital of £5,000, which was a huge fortune for those days. His brother was to pay him back as and when he earned it. Also his brother was to devote himself full-time to the business, while Lemon would give his time as and when he thought fit.[4] It would seem that one of his abiding interests remained the Penzance community, as can be seen from the various entries contained in the congregational minute books which still exist from that period.[5]

After an interim period of management by Lemon's nephews, Jacob James Hart and Frederick Hart,[6] his only son David (1799–1868) carried on his father's business

Poster by Ronald Searle.
[© Victoria & Albert Museum]

under the name of Lemon Hart & Son, and his descendants were to continue to trade in rum until Morris and Gilbey eventually bought the firm in 1879. The brand name survived successive mergers and takeovers, and after being part of the portfolio of United Rum Merchants, the brand today belongs to Allied Domecq.

When a French invasion was threatened, Hart raised a company of volunteers in Penwith to help in the defence of Cornwall against Napoleon, who prudently remained on the other side of the Channel. These were styled the Ludgvan Volunteers, and Mr. Hart was appointed their captain.[7] It was unusual for that period to find Jews among the militia.

As already mentioned, Lemon Hart was an active and committed member of the Penzance Synagogue and its community. Even after he had left Penzance for London, he continued his involvement, as for example when he engaged the Rev. B.A. Simmons as a *shochet* (ritual slaughterer) for the community in December 1811. Hart sent two letters of reference with the applicant: one was a recommendation from 'The High Priest Solomon Hirshell', a humorous reference to the Chief Rabbi of that period, and the other was his own recommendation, dated 23rd December 1811 to Mr. Hyman Woolf, his brother-in-law and the president of the congregation saying, "Annexed you have the *shochet* for the *Shul* (synagogue) I hired for you. He is a respectable young man and I hope you will behave to him properly, for you may rest assured those articles are very scarce in this market."[8] His hopes were not to be fulfilled, as Simmons was to have ongoing problems with the congregation.

A page in the minute book of the Penzance Synagogue dated to October 1809[9] records the following:

> We the congregation of this town do hereby agree from motives of benevolence and charity towards [name written in almost indecipherable Hebrew, but possibly Reb Leib Hena,[10] an infirm old man] to subscribe the sum of seven shillings per week for his maintenance to be paid in the proportions written opposite our respective names. We do hereby authorise Mr. L. Hart to pay him that sum weekly, on our credit which donations are to be reimbursed to said Mr. Hart agreeable to our respective shares when he thinks proper to demand the same in consideration of this allowance [Reb Leib Hena] is to be at Penzance every night if possible to prevent any accident happening to him from travelling to distant places.

The entry is in Lemon Hart's own hand, and his is the first of the five signatures appended to the entry. His share of the weekly stipend to be paid out was two shillings.

On 19th October 1810,[11] another entry records him as presenting various articles to the congregation. They included a *Sefer Torah* (Scroll of the Law) that had formerly belonged to Mr. Lazarus Solomon deceased (his father-in-law), a pair of silver hands for reading from the *Torah*, six large brass candlesticks, two large chandeliers and one curtain of red satin with white borders. Presumably, the latter was a curtain to hang in front of the Ark. In 1811, he donated a *Sefer Torah*, and pointer, a *megillah* (Scroll of Esther) and a *shofar* (a ram's horn, which was blown on the High Holidays). This proof of the existence of various artefacts (and there are other references showing that there was a reasonable abundance of scrolls and ritual appurtenances), make it all the sadder that there is no trace of even a single object today. Everything would seem to have vanished without a trace when the congregation was dissolved and the synagogue sold.

Lemon Hart had one son, David, who married a Cornish, non-Jewish girl. As for Lemon's four daughters, two married out of the Jewish religion. They were the issue of his first wife, Letitia (or Letty) Michael, of Swansea,[12] who met a horrific death. As the *Monthly Illustrated Journal* reported:

> On Sunday evening, Oct. 2nd, 1803, as Mrs. Hart, wife of Mr. Lemon Hart, spirit merchant, Penzance, was in an upper room alone, with a candle, her clothes unfortunately caught fire, and burnt her in a shocking manner. She was pregnant, has since been prematurely delivered, and now lies in a situation so deplorable, that her life is despaired of. In addition to this calamity, Mr. Lazarus Hart, father of the above-named Mr. Hart, died a few days ago in a fit of apoplexy. – (Mrs Hart died Monday, Oct. 10th).

The headline read, "Accidents seldom come alone, even in Penzance."[13]

He took as his second wife, Mary Solomon, of Goodman's Fields, London. They had no children. He died in Brighton at number 20 Marine Parade on 13th October 1845 and was buried two days later in the Brady Street cemetery in London.[14] Almost exactly seven years later, on 24th October 1852, Mary, whose Hebrew name was Miriam, died at 14 Euston Place, Euston Square, London and was buried in the same cemetery.[15]

NOTES

[1] Taken from advertising material relating to the history of United Rum Merchants Ltd.
[2] I am grateful to George Rigal for drawing my attention to the relevant insurance policies.
[3] According to information supplied by Godfrey Simmons in a letter dated 31st March 1998.
[4] ibid.
[5] In the Cecil Roth Collection in the Brotherton Library at the University of Leeds.
[6] They were the sons of Lemon Hart's sister Rebecca, who married Lazarus Jacobs, but they used the Hart surname.
[7] From a letter written by the maternal great-grandson of Lemon Hart, Geoffrey H. White to Cecil Roth on 25th February 1955. Cecil Roth Collection op. cit.
[8] Original letter in Godfrey Simmons's archive.
[9] op. cit.
[10] Victor Tunkel suggests that the surname Hena could derive from Hanau, a city in Hesse. The spelling in the minute book is Yiddish and if Reb Leib came from a Hanau family, he may well have adopted or been given 'Hena' as a cognomen.
[11] op. cit.
[12] Geoffrey H. White op. cit.
[13] From the *Monthly Illustrated Journal* of November, 1868.
[14] Great Synagogue section, Ba'aley Batim, 1796–1858.
[15] ibid.

Solomon Alexander Hart RA 1806–1881

JULIA WEINER

The place of Solomon Alexander Hart is secured in any book on Jewish artists as the result of his having been the first unequivocally Anglo-Jewish artist to achieve renown as an artist and to be elected a full member of the Royal Academy of Arts. Most of these volumes, however, dedicate only a few lines to him and it is his paintings of synagogue scenes that are usually referred to, fine examples being on display in the Jewish Museums of London and New York.[1] During his lifetime it was instead his history paintings which were best known, but today, though many are in public collections, their monumental size and poor condition means that they are rarely on view.[2]

Whilst Hart was certainly considered a celebrity in the Jewish world, whose almost every move was reported in the *Jewish Chronicle*, he was also an important member of the English art establishment who loyally served the Royal Academy from his election as Royal Academician until his death, refusing to be deflected by incidents of anti-Semitism he came across from fellow-members. In addition he was Curator of The Painted Hall at Greenwich, his services were regularly called on by the British Museum and South Kensington Museum, he acted as an examiner in art subjects in London and the provinces, and wrote regular art reviews in a number of periodicals. It was not surprising therefore that on his death in 1881 the *Jewish Chronicle* praised "the service that Mr Hart has rendered to our nation by consistently and unswervingly keeping the dignity of its race before the eyes of the art world."[3]

Solomon Alexander Hart was born in Plymouth in April 1806. His family had long established themselves in this city, for his great-great-grandfather Samuel Hart was a doctor whose portrait hung in the city's Cottonian Library.[4] The little that is known of his early life and family comes from his unfinished memoirs, which were published the year after his death by Alexander Brodie.[5] There he indicates that he inherited his artistic talent from his father, also Samuel Hart, who had been apprenticed to Abraham Daniel, a native of Bath, a jeweller, engraver and miniature painter.

Hart Senior obviously achieved some success as an engraver and he is mentioned as a mezzotint engraver in Bromley's *History of Engravers*, but his ambition was to enter the Royal Academy Schools. With this in mind, he came to London to study drawing, and took advice from James Northcote RA, a fellow Plymouth man who was to provide the same service later for his son. Unfortunately, he failed to qualify for studentship at the RA Schools, and gave up his artistic aspirations and returned home to marry. Nevertheless, "he left London with a fervent hope that he might some day have a son to follow that successfully in which he had failed."[6]

Hart does not mention his mother in his *Reminiscences*, but there is a suggestion that she died when he was young, since his father remarried whilst he was still at school. He appears to have had two brothers, one of whom, Mark Mordecai, became an engraver who sometimes made engravings of his brother's paintings; the other, Charles, emigrated to Baltimore.

Solomon Alexander Hart was first sent to school in Exeter at the age of seven, but stayed only a short time, returning to Plymouth in 1814. As a Jew, he was debarred from entering the local grammar school, which was 'restricted to churchmen', so he was instead taught by the Unitarian minister Rev Israel Worsley for five years. His new stepmother seems to have been pre-occupied with the well-being of her young stepson, keeping him indoors for long periods at a time, suggesting that he may have been a sickly child. Hart took advantage of this 'constant seclusion indoors'[7] to paint and draw, and James Northcote was called to see this work and give advice on whether he had a talent worth pursuing. He encouraged the young boy, and an apprenticeship was sought, but Samuel Hart, whose business ventures had failed, could not afford to pay the apprenticeship premium to the eminent engraver Charles Warren. A place with another engraver was turned down because of the harsh terms and, following in his father's footsteps, Hart moved to London with his family in 1820 with a view to becoming a student at the Royal Academy Schools.

Hart may have left Devon at a young age, but he remained deeply proud of his native town, donating one of his major works to Plymouth in 1879, and bequeathing £1000 to the Jewish congregation there. There is evidence that he regularly visited the area, and his sketchbooks contain drawings of various locations in the city including two drawings of the synagogue.[8] In his *Reminiscences*, he devoted an entire chapter to 'Devon Artists', probably welcoming the opportunity to link himself to such celebrated names as Sir Joshua Reynolds who was born in Plympton. He did make some effort to mount local exhibitions of pictures, but found the locals indifferent to art.

In London, Hart spent time in the British Museum preparing drawings of the Elgin Marbles for his examination, which he passed in 1823.[9] Although his father seems to have found some work as a Hebrew teacher, Hart was still the main provider for the family, and in order that he could study by day, he took on a variety of other work to do at night to earn a living. These included colouring theatrical prints, making copies of the Old Masters in miniature on ivory, painting some portrait miniatures, and working as an engraver. Given that he, his father and his brother all worked as engravers, it is not surprising that Hart was more appreciative than other Royal Academicians of this skill, and supported the engravers in their attempts to be admitted to full membership of the Royal Academy. "I contended that they were artists. I also suggested that he [Henry Pickersgill RA] should feel grateful to men who would transmit to future times a knowledge of his works when the materials of which they were composed had long since perished."[10]

Hart's first exhibited work was a portrait miniature of his father, which was shown at the Royal Academy in 1826, though he admitted later that he 'was dissatisfied with it'.[11] A further portrait of a foreign gentleman was shown there in 1829, but after this Hart devoted his energies to painting scenes from history and literature. It was not until 1841 that he again exhibited a portrait at the Academy by which time he had been elected Royal Academician and had established his reputation. In that year, the subscribers to the Jews' Hospital at Mile End wished to have a portrait of their patron, HRH The Duke of Sussex KG, for their boardroom, and asked the sitter to choose an artist. His request to be painted by Hart led to a number of other portrait commissions from other Jewish communal organisations and prominent members of the community including Alderman Salomans MP (1852), Sir Anthony de Rothschild Bart. (1856), The Rt. Hon. David Salomons, Lord Mayor of London (1856), the Rev. Dr Adler, the Chief Rabbi (1857) and Sir Moses Montefiore whom he painted twice, first in 1848 and again in 1869. Hart was praised for the accuracy of his portraits,[12] but, despite the fact that portraiture must have provided a good income, he continued to concentrate on his history paintings.

Although an early sketchbook includes drawings of Judaica,[13] Hart first painted subjects of Jewish interest in 1830, when he submitted a scene from *Ivanhoe* entitled *Isaac of York in the donjon of the castle of Reginald Front de Boeuf* to the Royal Academy and *The Elevation of the Law*,[14] depicting a scene from the Polish Synagogue in London, was exhibited at the Suffolk Street Gallery. The latter was purchased by Mr Robert Vernon and proved so popular that Hart was offered 17 commissions as a result. It was clear that Hart was equally interested in Catholicism, and commissions included two paintings of Catholic subject matter, *English Roman Catholic Nobility Taking Communion in the Sixteenth Century* and *A Lady Taking the Veil*, together with a further synagogue painting.

However, he found it hard to make ends meet by relying on commissions since "the small sums I received for them could not pay for rent, taxes, food and clothing for three persons."[15] He therefore decided to concentrate instead on painting more ambitious works with a view of becoming an RA.[16] He also did not wish to be known only as a painter of religious subjects, stating "I felt confident that I could do something of a more definite character in the expression of human emotion and strong dramatic action."[17] He turned for inspiration to dramatic events from medieval and early modern history, as well as to Shakespeare, and his paintings became much bigger. Examples include *The quarrel scene between Cardinal Wolsey and the Duke of Buckingham* from Shakespeare's *Henry VIII* (1834), *Coeur de Lion and the Soldan Saladin* (1835), on the strength of which he was elected an Associate of the Royal Academy, and *Henry I receiving the intelligence of the shipwreck of his son* (1840). He crowded these canvases with figures, and though these may now appear somewhat stiff and posed, they were praised for their dramatic expression at the time.[18] Hart remained deeply committed to traditional modes of representation, deploring works that he considered vulgar. He was particularly critical of the work of the Pre-Raphaelites: "Their ambition is an unhealthy thirst, which seeks *notoriety* by means of mere conceit. Abruptness, singularity, uncouthness are the counters with which they play for fame. Their trick is to defy the principles of beauty and the recognised axioms of taste."[19]

A contemporary reviewer wrote of Hart that "he . . . carefully studies correctness of costume and executes with nicety and precision all the details",[20] as is evident from his sketchbooks filled with meticulous drawings of architectural details such as windows, panelling and fireplaces, and costumes copied from Holbein. He relates that for his painting *The Submission of the Emperor Barbarossa to Pope Alexander III*, he was aided by Cardinal Wiseman who showed him a collection of vestments and other church furniture. Despite these efforts, errors did creep into his work; for example, in his 1840 painting *An Early Reading of Shakespeare*, the characters are dressed in costumes that he may have copied from Holbein but which are definitely pre-Shakespearean, and the book they are studying is of medieval design. An expert in Judaica would also find fault with his painting *The Feast of the Rejoicing of the Law in the Synagogue of Leghorn*, for the *Torah* headpieces are of English rather than Italian style.

He was finally elected to full membership of the Academy in 1840, an event which he attributed to the admiration he received for his 1839 painting *Lady Jane Grey at the place of her Execution*. This monumental canvas measured 14 feet square and took him a year to paint, but was never sold. It remained rolled up for

40 years until he donated it to Plymouth in 1879 for display either in the Guildhall or the law courts.

Hart seems to have been on good terms with many of his fellow-academicians. Turner was a friend who, according to Hart, added to and improved his 1847 painting of *John Milton Visiting Galileo* by sketching Galileo's solar system in the background. He also had a particularly close relationship with David Roberts, a neighbour of his for many years in Fitzroy Square, whose successful depictions of the Middle East may have encouraged Hart to turn once more to scenes of Jewish ritual and to consider Old Testament subjects. Hart was in Camarthen when Roberts died, but the funeral was postponed to allow him to attend.

Hart was regularly consulted about questions of Judaism at the Athenaeum Club where he was a committee member. Prior to his journey to the Holy Land, Sir David Wilkie RA specifically visited Hart to meet other Jews and receive advice concerning his travels, commenting later that he had obtained more instruction at his rooms concerning the object he had in view than at any previous discussion on the subject.[21]

He occasionally encountered some anti-Semitism. The most quoted example is perhaps the manner in which Sir William Collins introduced him to his family. "This is Mr Hart whom we have just elected Academician . . . Mr Hart is a Jew and the Jews crucified our Saviour, but he is a very good man for all that, and we shall see something more of him now."[22] Hart admits he was "taken aback at this very singular style of introduction". On another occasion he related how, during a political discussion, he was told that, "being a member of the Ancient Race, I could have not strong feelings of patriotism. Thereupon I retorted that I was an Englishman and that I had a right to dwell in England as long as it suited me."[23]

Hart's most important contribution to the Royal Academy was as Librarian, a position that he held from 1864 until his death. He obviously took his duties far more seriously than his predecessors who seemed "to think their duties consisted chiefly in unlocking the cases, handing books to students, restoring them to their cases."[24] During his fifteen years of tenure, the number of volumes in the library increased from 3,000 to 4,500, and his catalogue was widely consulted. The *Athenaeum* sums up his importance in his obituary as follows: "He found a chaos and left a library."[25]

Despite his rise in British society, Hart remained a devout Jew throughout his life. He was a member of the Western Synagogue for 53 years, but for the last 25 years attended Portland Street Synagogue. He was once asked how he could reconcile his profession with the fact that it was in direct contravention of the Second

Commandment – "Thou shalt not make to thyself any graven images" – replying that 'I pointed out that the context went on to say, not only that you should not make to yourself any graven image, but that you should not fall down and worship it and that I did not believe that anything I could paint would induce others, any more than myself to worship it."[26] His prominence in the art world led to a greater interest in the subject from other members of the community. In 1854, Hart was appointed Professor of Painting at the Royal Academy, a position he held until 1863 and over the years gave a number of lectures, which received great praise and were regularly published in the *Athenaeum*. The *Jewish Chronicle* noted that "several co-religionists, eminent for station, learning and taste" attended these lectures.[27]

Once he had established his name as a history painter, Hart turned once more to religious subjects, though he remained as interested in Catholic ritual as Jewish. In 1841, encouraged by the Duke of Sussex, he visited Italy where he made an elaborate series of drawings of architectural interiors, which he originally intended for publication but instead used for paintings. These included interiors of the cathedrals at Pisa and Modena and dinnertime in the refectory of the Convent of the Ognissanti, Florence. Two other paintings inspired by his travels are the aforementioned *Rejoicing of the Law in the Synagogue at Leghorn* and *The Scala Santa at the Benedictine Monastery of Subiaco, Near Rome*[28] which, though they show people of different religions at their devotions, reveal a remarkable similarity of treatment. In both, Hart shows great interest in the richly embroidered costumes and lace being worn as well as to devotional objects such as *Torah* scrolls, Sabbath lamps and rosary beads. He also pays particular attention to architectural features, including an elaborate window in the former and the large flagstones in the latter. In 1865 he showed a pair of paintings that again illustrate his interest in both faiths: *Meditating on the Book of Ecclesiastes* and *Meditating on the works of Thomas à Kempis*.

One of Hart's most popular Jewish paintings was *The Sabbath Lamp* exhibited at the Royal Academy in 1868, which even inspired a poem.[29] The *Jewish Chronicle* left its readers in no doubt of the importance of his Jewish genre paintings:

> The choice of Jewish subjects and the treatment of them in an excellent manner are of high value in so far as regards the outward face which Judaism has to present to the world. It is well that [our fellow citizens] should understand and learn to appreciate the spirit of poetry which resides in and inspires these practices and observances; that they should know and recognise the fact that even in these material days we are not merely a material people but that the poetry of our traditions and our rites has not faded away utterly.[30]

The Conference between Manassah Ben Israel and Oliver Cromwell, Solomon Alexander Hart, 1873. Destroyed in the Second World War.

In 1873, he exhibited the first of two history paintings depicting important events in Jewish history, *The Conference Between Manassah Ben Israel and Oliver Cromwell 1655*. Hart obviously greatly respected Cromwell, to the point that he had criticised a painting exhibited at the Royal Academy showing *The Protector contemplating the Crown* for presenting "a sorry compliment to the memory of a man whose splendid talents are every day rising into truer estimation."[31] His painting may have been inspired by the desire to publicise the role that Cromwell played in allowing Jews to settle in England, and he displayed his usual attention to detail, copying Cromwell from a portrait in Cambridge and using Rembrandt's print of Manassah Ben Israel. The success that this work received inspired him to contrast it with a less happy event from Jewish history, *The Proposal of the Jews to Ferdinand and Isabella (to secure their continued residence in Spain) to defray the expenses of the Moorish War rejected through the intolerance of Torquemada* which was exhibited in 1879.[32]

Hart continued to exhibit regularly at the Royal Academy until his death, but even the *Jewish Chronicle* was forced to admit that "the result of the painstaking exertions of his latter years indicated that the time had come when the reputation of the artist was to be regarded only in connection with his earlier works and would evidently not be increased by those of a later date."[33] He died at his home on 11th June 1881 and was buried at the Western Synagogue cemetery, his funeral attended by prominent representatives both of the Jewish community and of the Royal Academy including its president, Sir Frederick Leighton. A poem was published in his memory in the *Jewish Chronicle*,[34] and there was a proposal to found a lasting memorial in his name to encourage future generations of Jewish artists. In addition, the Royal Academy purchased a self-portrait of the artist for their collection.

There can be no doubt that Hart's success at the Royal Academy set a precedent and encouraged other talented young Jews to study there. During his lifetime, brothers Abraham and Simeon Solomon and Solomon J. Solomon (no relation) all gained admission to the Royal Academy Schools. Perhaps his greatest legacy was that the British art world had become accustomed to having a Jew in their midst, as is indicated by the regret expressed in *Punch* magazine in 1890 when the Russian Imperial Academy of Arts passed a law prohibiting Jews. "If such as rule, or rather such an exception could have been possible in England . . . what a discouragement it would been for all RAs who would thereby have *lost Hart*!"[35] The writer suggested that the Royal Academy write to its Russian counterpart to protest. By ensuring that Jewish artists were accepted into the highest echelons of the art world, Solomon Alexander Hart had also ensured that no such restrictive measures would be adopted in Britain.

NOTES

[1] *The Feast of Rejoicing of the Law in the Synagogue of Leghorn, Italy*, 1850 is in the Jewish Museum, New York, and *The Procession of the Law* is in the Jewish Museum, London.

[2] For example, *Lady Jane Grey at the place of her Execution* is in the collection of Plymouth Art Gallery, and *The Submission of the Emperor Barbarossa to Pope Alexander III* is in the Russell Cotes Art Gallery in Bournemouth.

[3] Obituary, *Jewish Chronicle*, 17th June 1881.

[4] Letter from Lewis Hyman of Plymouth published in the *Jewish Chronicle*, 13th November 1881.

[5] *Reminiscences of S.A. Hart*, edited by A. Brodie, London 1882.
[6] op cit. 5 p. 8.
[7] op cit. 5 p. 9.
[8] Now in the collection of the Royal Academy of Arts, London.
[9] An early sketchbook which includes drawings of the Elgin Marbles is now in the Victoria and Albert Museum.
[10] op cit. 5 p. 82.
[11] op cit. 5 p. 12.
[12] The portrait of the Chief Rabbi is described as "displaying a great deal of power and truth of expression, characteristic of the individual", *Jewish Chronicle* 31st July 1857 and the second portrait of Sir Moses Montefiore, commissioned for Ramsgate Town Hall, is described as "an admirable likeness, accurately drawn", *Jewish Chronicle*, 21st May 1869.
[13] Sketchbook in the Victoria and Albert Museum.
[14] This painting is now in the Tate Gallery collection but is sadly in extremely poor condition.
[15] op cit. 5 p. 17.
[16] op cit. 5 p. 17.
[17] op cit. 5 p. 13.
[18] The *Art Journal*, reviewing Hart's history paintings in Lord Northwick's Gallery, reported that they were hung amongst works by the greatest Old Masters, but that "the English painter thoroughly held his own amongst such a company of giants." Quoted in Hart's obituary, *Jewish Chronicle* 17th June 1881.
[19] The *Athenaeum*, June 1st 1850.
[20] *A History of the Royal Academy of Arts* by William Sandby, London, 1862, Vol. II, p. 167.
[21] op cit. 5 p. 70.
[22] op cit. 5 p. 74.
[23] op cit. 5 p. 143.
[24] op cit. 5 p. 83.
[25] Obituary, The *Athenaeum*, 18th June 1881.
[26] op cit. 5 p. 69.
[27] *Jewish Chronicle*, 23rd February 1855.
[28] Now in the collection of the Victoria and Albert Museum.
[29] Published in the *Jewish Chronicle*, 14th November 1873.
[30] *Jewish Chronicle*, 31st July 1868.
[31] *Athenaeum*, 1849 p. 575.
[32] Both this painting and *The Conference Between Manassah Ben Israel and Oliver Cromwell 1655* were presented to Jews' College and destroyed during the Second World War.

[33] *Jewish Chronicle*, obituary 17th June 1881.
[34] *Jewish Chronicle*, 17th June 1881.
[35] *Punch*, quoted in the *Jewish Chronicle*, 3rd January 1890.

Ezekiel Abraham Ezekiel of Exeter

FRANK GENT

It was in the 1750s that the first Ashkenazi (of German tradition) Jewish families settled in Exeter, notably the brothers Abraham and Benjamin Ezekiel. We do not know their town of origin, and their surname bears the hallmark of being a straightforward patronymic in the Jewish tradition of naming: Abraham the son of Ezekiel, and Benjamin the son of Ezekiel; a practice made clear by the names given to Abraham's famous son: Ezekiel Abraham Ezekiel i.e. Ezekiel the son of Abraham, the son of Ezekiel. One of the founders of the congregation was this Abraham Ezekiel, variously described as a silversmith,[1] and "for fifty years and upwards a respectable tradesman of Exeter".[2]

Five Jews had shops in the fashionable shopping area of Exeter sufficiently well established to warrant inclusion in the *Exeter Pocket Journal* of 1796. The latter recorded that there were two silversmiths, an engraver who sold a variety of goods, a pawnbroker, and a stationer. The trades followed by these early immigrants were typical of middle-class Jews in the eighteenth century. Barred from professions, and susceptible to persecution, they needed occupations that were mobile, transportable and transferable. Silversmithing was consequently popular with those who could afford the apprenticeship and the basic resources.

By 1757 the nascent community had followed tradition in acquiring a plot of land in which to bury its dead as a priority before the construction of a synagogue. The burial ground at Bull Meadow, still used and maintained by the Jewish congregation of Exeter, lies just outside the Roman wall of the city, near the South Gate, opposite the Wynards Almshouses, in Magdalen Road. The lease was issued to "Abraham Ezekiel of the parish of St Kerrian in the city of Exon, silversmith". The charge was five shillings, and in return the Jews received a plot of land 80 feet long and 22 feet wide. The lease was for 99 years, and a traditional Devonshire 'lease for three lives': "if the said Abraham Ezekiel aged thirty one years, Rose his daughter aged two years and Israel Henry the son of Henry Israel aged two years any or either of them shall happen so long to live." The annual rent was ten shillings and six pence payable in four instalments quarterly. In addition, Abraham Ezekiel was required to build a wall of brick, stone or cob, with coping, eight feet high around the plot. This lease was revised and reissued on 17th January, 1803. The three lives were now "Solomon Ezekiel son of Ezekiel Benjamin Ezekiel (son of Benjamin Ezekiel) of Newton Abbot in the county of Devon silversmith, now aged about seventeen years, Simon Levy son of Emanuel Levy of the city of Exeter silversmith, now aged about twelve years, and Jonas Jonas son of Benjamin Jonas of Plymouth Dock in the said county silversmith now aged about twelve years". The rent remained the same: ten shillings and sixpence annually in quarterly instalments. The new lease of 24th September, 1827 was issued to "Henry Ezekiel (son of Abraham Ezekiel) of the said city of Exeter gentleman, Isaac Solomon of the same city silversmith, Jacob Jacobs of the same city pen manufacturer, Simon Levy of the parish of St Thomas in the county of Devon working silversmith, and Morris Jacobs of the same city silversmith". The 'lives' were "Solomon Ezekiel now aged about forty one years and son of Ezekiel Benjamin Ezekiel of Newton Abbot in the county of Devon silversmith, Simon Levy now aged about thirty six years and son of Emanuel Levy of the city of Exeter silversmith, and Jonas Jonas now aged about thirty six years and son of Benjamin Jonas of Plymouth Dock silversmith". The rent was again increased, to two pounds and two shillings annually.

An important turning point was reached on 5th November 1763, when Abraham Ezekiel and Kitty Jacobs obtained a lease for a "parcel of ground in the parish of St Mary Arches" on which the present Exeter Synagogue was built. The ceremony marking the opening of the synagogue on 10th August 1764 has fortuitously been recorded.

Ezekiel Abraham Ezekiel's father and uncle, Abraham and Benjamin Ezekiel, came as young men in their twenties, probably from the Rhineland, and settled in Exeter in the 1740s or early 1750s. Abraham was a silversmith and a watchmaker, respected for his craftsmanship, and recognised and accepted by the Exeter gentry and bourgeoisie.[3] He was a goldsmith but no work of his is known, except for a pocket watch, which was formerly at the Royal Albert Memorial Museum, Exeter, but is now lost. He and his wife Sarah, who died in Exeter in June 1806 aged 70, had six children, including two sons, Henry Ezekiel and Ezekiel Abraham Ezekiel. Similarly respected was his brother Benjamin whose untimely death in October 1785 earned him the unusual honour of a brief obituary in the *Flying Post*: "Last week died suddenly, as he was walking near St Bartholomew's yard, Mr Benjamin Ezekiel, for many years a respectable inhabitant of this city. . ."

Ezekiel Abraham Ezekiel was born in Exeter in 1757, the eldest of at least six children: his sisters Rosa, Anna, Catherine and Amelia, his brother Henry, and a daughter whose name is unknown but whose death was reported in the *Flying Post* on 16th September, 1790. In 1772, at the age of fifteen, he was apprenticed to Alexander Jenkins, an Exeter goldsmith, for a premium of £45. Presumably he continued to live with his parents so that he could keep the requirements of his Jewish faith. It was towards the end of this apprenticeship that he produced his first engraving, a view of Bideford. The advertisement on 23rd July 1779 read thus:

> A Perspective View of Bideford is just published by Subscription. Engraved by Ezekiel. Sold by Mr Henry Mugg, Bookseller, and the Engraver, at Mr Ezekiel's, Silversmith, Exon; also by Mr John Jewell the Author, at Bideford, by whom Youth are genteelly Boarded and instructed in all the Branches of Practical Mathematics. Price 10s 6d in Colours 12s 6d.

The print is listed in Somers Cocks' catalogue of Devon topographical prints, along with another engraving by Ezekiel of Tapley House, but no copies of either appear to be held by any of the local or national collections. There is still a painting in the Royal Hotel, Bideford, which is said to be John Jewell's original work. A letter to the present owner of Tapley House confirmed Ezekiel's authorship, and established beyond doubt both the authorship and the quality of the work, and the fact that the view of Bideford and the view of Tapley occur on the same engraving.

Ezekiel's education is unknown, but he was fluent in English, Hebrew and German. In 1784 his premises were opposite the George Inn in North Street, just round the corner from the synagogue, and he presumably succeeded his father who left his wife and retired to live with his daughter Rosa in Portsmouth. He was a versatile artist,[4] but his prints were not always a commercial success, and he advertised his engravings of Bideford and Mr John Patch at reduced prices:

> The large Perspective view of Bideford, engraved by him from a Drawing by Mr. Jewell, to be had, Price Five Shillings.[5]

Self-taught, he had produced the latter while apprenticed to a jeweller, from a drawing by Jewell.[6]

The British Museum has four examples of his work – a portrait of Micaiah Towgood (1700–92), dissenting minister of Exeter, engraved in line after Opie, and published in 1787; a stipple engraving of the same portrait published in 1794; a portrait of John Patch, surgeon at Exeter, engraved in line and stipple after Opie, and published in 1789, and a stipple engraving of the portrait of General Stringer Lawrence (1697–1775) by Sir Joshua Reynolds, published in 1795. The Royal Albert Memorial Museum possesses copies of his engravings of the portrait of Thomas Glass, physician at Exeter, published 1788; a portrait of the Rev. John Marshall, schoolmaster at Exeter, after Keenan, published in 1798 on which he is

Engravings by Ezekiel: *Micaiah Towgood*, 1787, after Opie.

General Stringer Lawrence, 1795, after Reynolds. [both: British Museum]

described as 'engraver, optician and goldsmith'. Another engraving by him was entitled *The Breastplate of the 3rd Exeter Volunteer Corps embodied in 1800*. Fincham records fourteen ex-libris signed by Ezekiel. A miniature painting of a young woman, said to be his sister, and attributed to Ezekiel by the late Basil Long, is also in the Royal Albert Memorial Museum, Exeter.

In February 1784 he placed a large advertisement in the *Flying Post* listing his skills:

> . . . by constant Supply of new Patterns from London, executes Perspective and Ornamental Copper-Plate Engraving, Shop Cards, Draughts, Bills of Exchange, Household Plate, Seals in Steel, Silver, and Stone, Merchants and all other stamps, in the newest and most elegant taste:- Neat Copper Plate Printing, on reasonable Terms, Jewellery Work in general, with curious Devices in Hair, done in the most pleasing Manner. Mourning Rings and all Funereal Engraving, on the shortest Notice.

He engraved many bookplates, some fourteen of which are recorded in publications. He also produced a great many trade cards, and the Victoria and Albert Museum has Ezekiel's own trade card, a fine example of the engraver's art, dating from c.1797 and adorned with cherubs engaged in various branches of the arts and sciences. His finest works are his portraits: *Thomas Glass* in 1788, *John Patch* in 1789, *Major General Stringer Lawrence*, c.1790, *Micaiah Towgood*, 1794, *William Holwell* (this one I have not traced), *John Marshall*, 1798.

He also engraved the masthead used for a while by the *Flying Post*, the title page and a map for Dunsford's *Tiverton*, and the breastplate of the Third Exeter Volunteer Corps. These engravings are amongst the best produced in the medium, and almost all are of local interest. In 1795 he started to deal in optical instruments; and also moved his shop to a new location seven doors below North Street in Fore Street, with his brother Henry's help. In 1795 he added to his already considerable repertoire of skills that of optician, claiming to have studied the science with an expert, and to be the first of the profession in the West Country. He was no mere dispenser, but rapidly added telescopes, microscopes, fossils and mineralogy to his range. The microscope with slides displayed in the museum in Exeter is a tribute to his skills.

E.A. Ezekiel of Exeter published a trade card in 1796 by which he informed the public that besides being an engraver and optician he was a goldsmith and printseller, and sold spectacles, telescopes, quadrants, cutlery, plate, gold seals, watches, prints and materials for drawing.

In 1800, he "respectfully informs the public, and particularly the Gentry who may visit this City at the ensuing Assizes, that he has just fitted up a large selection of Optics, viz. Spectacles mounted in silver, tortoiseshell and steel . . . reading glasses, Claude Lorraines, opera glasses, achromatic telescopes, magic lanterns, microscopes . . . wheel and pedement barometers and thermometers . . . for the hothouse or brewery."[7]

He was a successful miniature painter, which he took up at the age of 40,[8] carrying on at the same time the trade of engraving in addition to the business of a silversmith and scientific optician.[9] In 1799 he advertised his further talent as miniaturist, and achieved quite a reputation in this field. Only one such work by him appears to be extant, a portrait of a young woman now in the collection of the Royal Albert Memorial Museum, Exeter, though others are mentioned in family papers. His own portrait was exhibited at the end of the last century, at the Anglo-Jewish Historical Exhibition of 1887, but its whereabouts are now unknown.[10] In the manner of the time, and to his credit, Ezekiel passed on his skills to an apprentice. He first advertised for one in May 1790: "As Genius will be the principal Premium required, it is expected that none will apply but such who possess a real Turn for Drawing, and Skill in Penmanship." Other advertisements followed. 15/10/1801: Peace! German translations. 10/3/1803: Dollands telescopes. 17/3/1803: naval sabres. He advertised again in June 1805, but by now he was already a sick man, a fact noted by the Militia List, discharging him for reasons of health from any possible military service in the war with France.

Just eighteen months later, when Ezekiel died of dropsy after a long illness on 13th December 1806, the *Exeter Flying Post* printed the following obituary:

> On Saturday last died aged 48, Mr. E.A. Ezekiel, of this city, engraver and jeweller. He had long lingered under the complaint of dropsy and contemplated his dissolution with a most religious resignation. He was followed to the grave by many respectable persons, who have for several years passed enjoyed the pleasure of his agreeable conversation, and the attachment of his unshaken friendship. In the profession of an engraver, he possessed a correct taste, a happy facility in making designs, to meet the ideas of his employers, and as a workman, he was certainly unequalled out of London: his portraits of several distinguished characters in this city and neighbourhood, will always be admired for their faithful execution: they never fail to excite the reward due to his merit, while they renew the presence of a person whose likeness he represented, with great correctness. In a word there are few men whose loss will be more felt, not only by his immediate friends and connections, but also by the public at large. A discourse was delivered at the grave, previous to the interment, by the chief priest of the Synagogue; who, truly and affectingly, held up the deceased as a pattern for imitation, both as a good son and brother, a good man, and a good citizen of the world.

This was a remarkable testimonial to his standing in the town, with a reputation achieved whilst constantly and proudly maintaining his Jewishness, and that this obituary was no mere ephemeral flattery can be seen from the fact that Ezekiel's name was listed as late as 1830 among *A List of Persons of Eminence, Genius and Public Notoriety, Natives of Exeter*, a series of biographies of distinguished Exonians written by George Oliver, a remarkable Roman Catholic priest and scholar.

The obituary also gives some clues to his private life: Ezekiel died unmarried, and in his will requested that the minister, the Rev. Moses Levy, say *kaddish* for him, normally a son's duty. His family life had not always been happy – it appears from his will and other evidence that his parents had separated some years before his death, the father going to live with his daughter Rosy in Portsmouth, dying there in 1799, aged 73. His mother Sarah died in Exeter in 1806 at the age of 70. For her pains Rosy was cut off by her brother with a shilling, whilst another sister, Anne, received five pounds in recognition of her "great attention of duty to our dear mother and to me". Ezekiel spent his adult life living with his unmarried brother Henry and maiden sisters Kitty and Amelia at their shop at 179 Fore Street, and they continued the business after his death. He had passed on his artistic skills to his pupil, and presumably former apprentice, C. Frost. His artistic genius met with some financial success: at his death his estate was valued at just less than £600. He left eight pounds to the synagogue for the purchase of a clock with a commemorative inscription on the dial, which sadly has not survived.

His brother Henry, although a watchmaker, lacked his elder brother's genius as an artist, but was evidently more successful financially: "Providence having blessed him with a competency and happy prospect in life, any small legacy is unnecessary, but as a small remembrance I bequeath to him all my Hebrew and English books. . ."

A further indication of the amicable relationship which apparently prevailed is the employment by Jewish shopkeepers and tradesmen of non-Jews as pupils and assistants. After E.A. Ezekiel's death, "James Rickard, Engraver, pupil to the late Mr Ezekiel of this city . . . informs the public . . . that he intends carrying on the above business"[11] and "C. Frost, senior pupil of the late E.A. Ezekiel . . . solicits the patronage. . . ."[12] It looks as though Ezekiel himself had been the pupil of one J. Woodman, because he had advertised in somewhat similar terms on the death of Woodman in 1784.[13]

Henry was married just three years after his brother's death on Wednesday 14th March 1810 in Exeter to Betsy Levy, daughter of the synagogue minister, Moses Horwitz Levy. Henry was 38 and his wife ten years his junior. She bore him three daughters, all of whom married. Henry died in 1835, leaving properties and investments. The portraits of himself and his wife Betsy in the Jewish Museum in London show a wealthy, middle-class couple in their prime. The two maiden sisters, Kitty (Catherine) and Amelia, continued to run the business until 1837 when Catherine died aged 69 on July 3rd, soon after the death of her brother Henry on November 10th 1836, and Amelia died on 6th June, 1839, at East Teignmouth, aged 60. They too had lacked the artistic skills of their illustrious brother, and soon after his death abandoned the engraver's equipment, advertising in 1810 and 1812 "a rolling press to be disposed of". After Ezekiel's death, his brother Henry presented proof impressions of his brother's engravings to the Devon and Exeter Institution in the Cathedral Close, and there most of them still hang in the entrance hall, a fitting reminder of one of the most talented sons of Exeter and its Jewish community.

List of Work attributed to Ezekiel Abraham Ezekiel

Those whose whereabouts are no longer known are marked with an asterisk.

1779, July 23rd *View of Bideford*, Tapley House
1786 Trade card Dartmouth, BM Banks 1.95
1788 Trade card Thompson's Hotel, BM Banks 1.113
1788, March 20th *Thomas Glass*, RAMM
1789, September 1st *Mr John Patch*, RAMM
*1789 *Rev Micaiah Towgood* [line engraving] [EFP 23rd February, 1792], BM
1789, September 10th Banner *Exeter Flying Post*, WCSL
1790 Frontispiece Dunsford's *Tiverton*, WCSL
1790 Map of Tiverton (Dunsford), WCSL
1792 Trade card Brewer, BM Banks 131.6
1794, March 1st *Rev Micaiah Towgood* [stipple], BM
1795 *General Stringer Lawrence*, BM
*c.1795 *Mr William Holwell*, N&G
c.1797 Trade card, V & A
1798 January 12th *Rev. John Marshall*, RAMM
1801 Medal, Topsham Museum
*1801, February 2nd Four medals, EAO
*1801, February 17th Three medals, EAO
*1801, February 28th One medal, EAO
*1801, September 9th One seal, EAO
1803 *The General Apiarian* (title page), D&EI
1803 *The General Apiarian* (illustration), D&EI
1804 Banknote Baring, Jackson, Gould & Vicary, LBA
c.1806 Banknote Exeter Bank, NWBA
N.D. Microscope, RAMM [75/1918]
N.D.* Breastplate 3rd Exeter Volunteers
N.D. Bookplate J. Bishop, Jewish Museum
N.D. Bookplate C. Chichester, BM
N.D. Bookplate N. Cooksley, BM
N.D. Bookplate Halloran, BM
N.D. Bookplate J. Hucks, BM
N.D. Bookplate Lawrence Hynes Halloran, BM
N.D.* Bookplate R. D(uncan)

N.D.* Bookplate Hall
N.D.* Bookplate S.L.
N.D.* Bookplate Major Humphrey Lawrence
N.D. Bookplate Edward Phillips, BM
N.D.* Bookplate Trefusis
N.D.* Bookplate Robert Weston
N.D. Bookplate J. W. Williams, BM
N.D.* Bookplate Wood
N.D. Bookplate Palk, BM
N.D. Bookplate (I Williams del), BM
N.D. Bookplate Wood, BM
N.D. Trade card London Inn, BM Banks 1.138
N.D. Trade card Burnett, BM Banks 84.15
N.D.* Trade card C. Upham, 62, High St, Exeter, N&G
N.D.* Trade card B. Hewer, Fore St, Exeter, N&G
N.D.* Trade card John Reynell, Fore St, Exeter, N&G
N.D.* Trade card Post Office, Exeter, N&G
N.D.* Trade card Hedgeland, Magdalen Street St, Exeter, N&G
N.D.* Trade card Dix & Son, Exe Lane, Exeter, N&G
N.D.* Trade card Arundell's, St Sidwell's, Exeter, N&G
N.D.* Trade card John Ferris & Co, Fore St, Exeter, N&G
N.D.* Trade card Jane Alway, Moretonhampstead, N&G
N.D. Miniature of sister, RAMM

Abbreviations:

BM: British Museum Department of Prints and Drawings
D&EI: Devon and Exeter Institution Library
EAO: Exeter Assay Office (Devon Record Office)
LBA: Lloyds Bank Archives
N&G: *Devon & Cornwall Notes and Gleanings*, III. 35 pp. 167–8, 15th November, 1890
NWBA: National Westminster Bank Archives
RAMM: Royal Albert Memorial Museum, Exeter
V&A: Victoria and Albert Museum
WCSL: West Country Studies Library, Exeter

NOTES

1. *Exeter Pocket Journal*, 1791.
2. *Sherborne and Yeovil Mercury*, 2nd December 1799.
3. See his obituary in the *Hampshire Repository*, II, 20th November 1790, quoted by C. Roth in *TJHSE*, XIII, 1936, and p. 177.
4. See Rubens 'Further Notes on early Anglo-Jewish Artists', *TJHSE*, XVIII, 1953, plate 19, after p. 108.
5. *Trewman's Flying Post*, 5th February 1784.
6. *Notes and Queries*, Series II, vol. viii, p. 494.
7. *Trewman's Flying Post*, 13th March 1800, records a barometer made by him. For a similar advertisement by Joseph Abrahams, see *Trewman's Flying Post*, 17th January 1799.
8. *Devonshire Freeholder*, 12th July 1822.
9. Rubens, *Early Anglo-Jewish Artists*, p. 104 quoting G. Pycroft, *Art in Devonshire*, Exeter, 1883, p. 45.
10. Rubens, *Early Anglo-Jewish Artists*, p. 105.
11. *Trewman's Flying Post*, 18th December 1806.
12. ibid.
13. *Trewman's Flying Post*, 5th February 1784.

The Jews of Barnstaple

HELEN FRY

A fleeting reference in an obituary for Abraham Ralph in *The Gentleman's Magazine* of 1805 provides the first and only known reference to a worshipping Jewish community in Barnstaple in the eighteenth century. But for this, we could have assumed that there had been no active Jewish community in the town.[1] Evidence for Jewish traders in the town can be found in trade directories, but no direct mention of a place for worship until this 1805 reference, which reads:

> Mr. Abraham Ralph, silversmith of Barnstaple, Devon, where he was the oldest shopkeeper and had been in business upwards of 40 years. The Synagogue assemblies were always held in his house.[2]

Records have so far not revealed a purpose-built synagogue in the town, but there were clearly enough Jewish men in the town and surrounding area to form a *minyan* to hold a full service for the Sabbath and High Holy Days. A room was converted for such purposes in Abraham Ralph's house. Much more about any active Jewish life in Barnstaple we cannot tell from these references.

Abraham Ralph was a local businessman who had lived and worked in the town for some 40 years. He is mentioned in *The Universal British Directory* for 1793–1798 as: "a silversmith and dealer in Wearing Apparel". The Jewish historian Cecil Roth comments that "Ralph provides us with yet another instance of the Jewish silversmith and watchmaker in the English country-town in the middle of the eighteenth century."[3] This is in contrast to the popular assumption that most Devon and Cornwall Jews were pedlars. Indeed some did follow that occupation, but many were in fact highly skilled craftsmen with the financial means to set themselves up in business.

His son, Leape Ralph (1770–1824), is described as a "Pawnbroker and engraver".[4] Leape, also known as Lewis or Judah, made a silver pointer for the Plymouth Synagogue in 1772.[5] He was married to Hannah Ralph,[6] who lies buried in the old Jewish cemetery on Plymouth Hoe.[7] Their children were Samuel (1803–67), Frederick (1804–50), Amelia (1812–74) and Abraham (1814–90). Lewis had worked as a silversmith as well as a Navy Agent in Plymouth in 1812.

A reference to another Barnstaple silversmith is to be found in an advertisement in the *Exeter Flying Post* of 26th May 1808:[8]

> TO be Sold by auction at the King's Arms, Barnstaple, on Tuesday next, the 31st of May instant, by the order of Mr. E. Levy, of Exeter, administrator to the effects of the late Isaac Wolfe, of Barnstaple, silversmith, deceased, all the said I. Wolfe's late STOCK in TRADE, consisting of various articles of silver and plated goods, watches, jewellery, etc., etc.
> The sale will begin at eleven o'clock in the afternoon.
> LEWIS LANGDON, Auctioneer.
> On the following days will be sold at the King's Arms aforesaid, a quantity of UNREDEEMED PLEDGES, the property of the above Mr. E. Levy.
> All persons who stand indebted to the estate of the Late Mr. Wolfe are requested forthwith to pay their accounts to Mr. Levy; and all persons to whom the deceased stood indebted are requested to send in the particulars of their demands to the said Mr. Levy, so that they may be examined and settled.

We know something of the lives of local Jews from original court documents relating to cases held in the Barnstaple courts.[9] Abraham Ralph was involved in a legal dispute with a foot soldier in 1765. He swore an affidavit before the Barnstaple court on 3rd March 1765 that Thomas Blackburn Phillips, a foot soldier of the Thirteenth Regiment, owed him the sum of seven pounds and fourteen shillings.[10] Interestingly, on the document Abraham had signed his name in Hebrew. Isaac Moses, silversmith of South Molton registered a similar case of money owing to a local Jewish trader at the courts, in August 1765.[11] He was owed the sum of two pounds, five shillings and seven pence halfpenny by William Brooks, a tanner in Barnstaple, who in turn took Isaac Moses to court and issued a warrant for trespass.[12] Two other local Jews were involved in court cases in the 1760s: Jonas Nathan in 1760[13] and Hart Levi in 1762.[14] Hart Levi, a pedlar, was accused of behaving in an 'indecent manner' towards Eleanor Gribble, the wife of Robert Gribble.

A portrait, now in private ownership, provides the final evidence of a local Jew. Betsy Levy (1759–1836), originally from Barnstaple, is known to have married Isaac Jacobs of Totnes in 1784.[15] Three of their sons married Abraham Ralph's three daughters.[16] As Susser has highlighted,[17] the portrait of Betsy is unusual in that, out of some twenty extant portraits of eighteenth- and nineteenth- century married Jewish women in Devon and Cornwall, she is the only one shown with her head covered, wearing a lace cap. In all the other portraits, the women have their heads uncovered. When she died in 1836, she was buried in the old Jewish cemetery on Plymouth Hoe.[18] In her will, she left a number of items to her children:

A diamond ring with eleven stones to her daughter Caroline, 6 silver spoons with her children's initials and a silver pepper caster with her name thereon to her daughter Rose, a silver chased cup to her son David (if he wants it); residue to her son Lewis and daughters Hannah and Caroline.[19]

To date, these are the only documentary records that have been located about local Barnstaple Jews. Much more than that, it is not possible to say unless further research uncovers new documentation. However, it is apparent that "the pioneers of these early Anglo-Jewish communities followed more dignified callings than was formerly imagined."[20]

NOTES

[1] It may not be possible to name more than six local families; cf. *The Jews of South-West England*, Bernard Susser, 1993, p. 51. For Jews born in Barnstaple, see *The Decennial Census 1841–1891*, Bernard Susser, 1995, pp. 15, 16 & 18.

[2] *The Gentleman's Magazine*, vol. LXXV, Pt2, 1805, p. 1176.

[3] *The Rise of Provincial Jewry*, Cecil Roth, 1964, p. 22.

[4] The *Universal British Directory* 1793–1798, vol. 2, Pt 1, pp. 313–5.

[5] Susser, op. cit. *The Jews of South-West England*, p. 218.

[6] Her Hebrew name was Gittle bat Zvi (Gittle the daughter of Zvi).

[7] Ref: B27 in *Tombstone Inscriptions in the Old Jewish Cemetery on Plymouth Hoe*, Bernard Susser, 2nd edition, 1996, p. 24. She died on the Sabbath in May 1853 at the age of 87.

[8] I am grateful to Frank Gent of the Exeter Hebrew Congregation for sharing with me this product of his own research.

[9] Records now held in the North Devon Record Office, Barnstaple.

[10] Ref: B1/3975, North Devon Record Office. I am grateful to Tim Wormleighton for drawing my attention to these documents.

[11] Ref: B/2981.

[12] Ref: B/2983.

[13] Ref: B/2816.

[14] Ref: B/2429.

[15] Susser, op. cit. *Tombstone Inscriptions*, pp. 13 & 16.

[16] Roth, op. cit. *The Rise of Provincial Jewry*, p. 22.

[17] Susser, op. cit. *The Jews of South-West England*, p. 223.

[18] Susser, op. cit. *Tombstone Inscriptions*, p. 16 Ref: A50.

[19] ibid.

[20] Roth, op. cit., p. 22.

Catalogue of Exhibition

Penlee House Art Gallery & Museum, Penzance	7/2/00–1/4/00
Royal Albert Memorial Museum, Exeter	13/5/00–17/6/00
Falmouth Art Gallery	12/8/00–28/10/00
Plymouth City Museum & Art Gallery	16/11/00–28/2/01
Museum of North Devon, Barnstaple	6/3/01–28/4/01

Lenders

Ben Uri Art Society, London
Brotherton Library, Leeds
Mrs. Jack Clarfelt, London
Courtney Library, Truro
Exeter Central Library
Exeter Hebrew Congregation
Evelyn Friedlander, London
Helen Fry, London
Frank Gent, Crediton
Mr. and Mrs. Tony Gilman, Penzance
Alex Jacob Archive
The Jewish Museum, London
Archive Service, Lloyds TSB Group
Museum of North Devon, Barnstaple
Penlee House Art Gallery and Museum, Penzance
Plymouth Hebrew Congregation
Royal Albert Memorial Museum, Exeter
Royal Cornwall Museum, Truro
Mr. and Mrs. Ivan Segal, Florida
Rev. Canon and Mrs. Richard Stranack, Bude
Bernard Susser Archive
Topsham Museum, Exeter
Peter Wadham, Exeter

1. *An Old Jew*
   John Opie (1761–1807)
   Oil on canvas
   c.1780
   H: 69.5 cm, W: 47.5 cm unframed
   The Royal Institution of Cornwall,
   the Royal Cornwall Museum, Truro

Hailed by Sir Joshua Reynolds as "the wondrous Cornishman", John Opie is considered to be the first Cornish artist of significance and certainly the first Cornish portraitist of renown.

Opie painted many portraits of people he encountered in his Cornish travels, so it can be assumed that this portrait is of a local Jew, painted before he went to London. There he became Professor of Painting at the Royal Academy, and on his death was buried in St. Paul's Cathedral. This was one of four paintings shown to but not purchased by George III. The idea was for Opie to show himself in his most Rembrandtesque manner and to convince the king that an English-born artist could paint old men and beggars in successful rivalry of Rembrandt.

67

2. The Bischofswerder Family
   Photograph c.1890
   Penzance
   H: 13.5 cm, W: 20 cm
   Victor Bishop, Norwich

This photograph shows members of the Bischofswerder family in Penzance with the retired minister of the congregation, Isaac Bischofswerder, seated on the right.

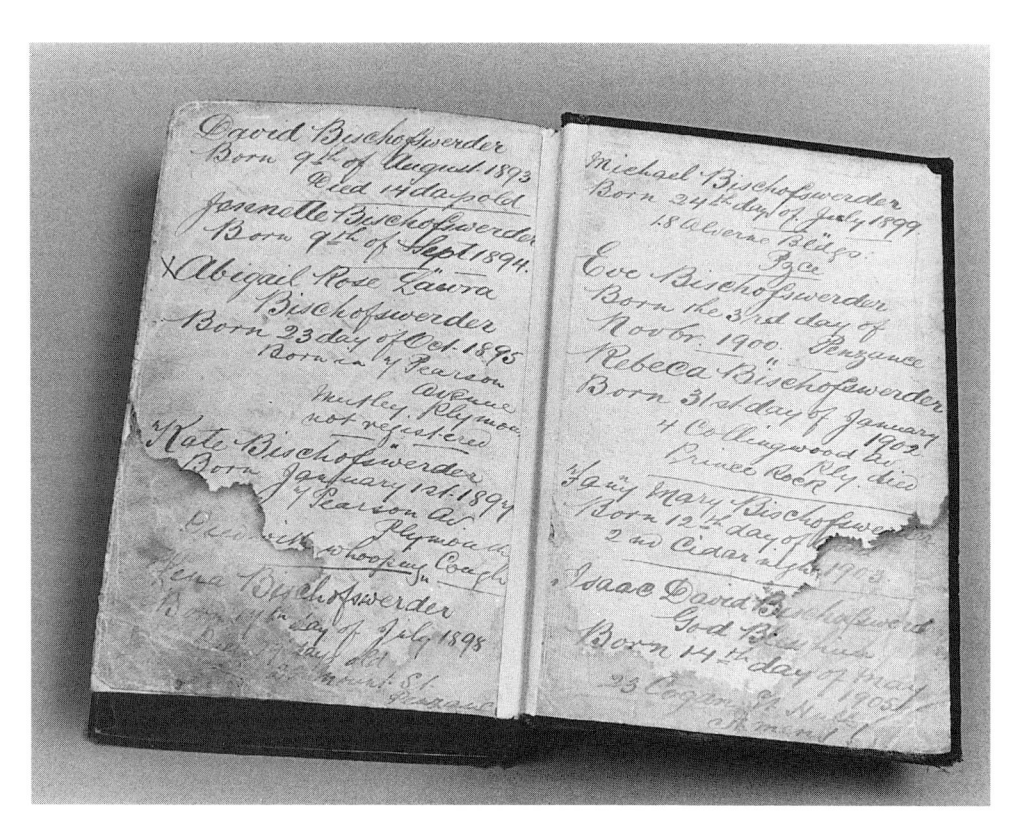

3. Bible from the Bischofswerder family
   Late nineteenth century
   Linen bound
   H: 26.2 cm, W: 20.5 cm
   Mr and Mrs Ivor Segal, Florida

This nineteenth-century edition of the Bible has lost its title page. Inside the front board, Marcus Bischofswerder wrote his address in Hull in 1906. Inside the back board (upside down), are recorded the dates of his birth in 1852 and that of his wife Sarah in 1864, followed by the names and dates of their 17 children, several of whom died in infancy. All these entries are in one hand. Various addresses are given, in both Penzance and Plymouth and ultimately Hull, suggesting a somewhat peripatetic life. Marcus was one of the sons of Isaac Bischofswerder who served as a rabbi in Penzance and was buried there in 1899.

4. Cover for the Torah (Mappa)
   1842
   Plymouth
   Red velvet edged with grey ribbon, embroidered with gold metal thread and backed with grey rough linen.
   H: 43 cm, W: 45 cm
   The Susser Archive

This textile would have been used to cover the Torah while it lay open on the reader's desk, but was not actually being read. The inscription reads, "This is donated by the honourable Samuel, son of the sage Chaim L(?) the holy congregation of Plymouth in the year 5602 (=1842) according to the minor calculation."

5. Plaque
   1784
   Plymouth
   Silver, no marks
   H: 18 cm, W: 13cm
   Plymouth Hebrew Congregation

This plaque is engraved, "Yechiel bar Zvi, David bar Shimshon (Cohen), Asher bar Zvi, Alexander bar Abraham, Samuel bar Zvi, Juspa bar Abraham, Jacob bar Mordecai. Judah bar Shimshon (Cohen), Asher bar Abram Zvi , the workers 4th Sivan (5)544 (=1784)." On the right of the plaque is written, "And all the work was completed on 4th Sivan". The left side reads, "Samuel bar Zvi and Jacob bar Mordecai".

The synagogue building was completed in 1761, but it would seem that the furnishings were completed in 1784. These same names appear on a silver pointer of 1783.

Literature: Bernard Susser, *The Jews of South-West England*, 1993, p. 218.

6. Torah Pointer
   1783
   Plymouth
   Silver, no marks
   L: 27 cm
   Plymouth Hebrew Congregation

The Torah pointer has a plain shaft and an octagonal handle, divided by a round knop with a matching finial. It bears the same names as the plaque, "Yechiel bar Zvi, David bar Shimshon (Cohen), Asher bar Zvi, Alexander bar Abraham, Samuel bar Zvi, Juspa bar Abraham, Jacob bar Mordecai. Judah bar Shimshon (Cohen), Asher bar Abram Zvi". The pointer would have been part of a set of the earliest extant ritual furnishings of the synagogue.

Literature: Bernard Susser, *The Jews of South-West England*, 1993, p. 218.

7. Rimmonim (Torah Finials or Bells)
   1783
   London
   Silver, parcel gilt, velvet, London assay mark, maker's mark IR
   H: 37 cm
   Plymouth Hebrew Congregation

The rimmonim are in the English style, with alternately concave and convex fluting in its layers. They are surmounted by crowns with a red velvet cushion, in the style of the secular beadles' and sheriffs' staves in the City of London. For England, the idea of putting the bells out at a distance from the body of the finials was revolutionary.

Literature: Bernard Susser, *The Jews of South-West England* 1993, p. 220. Jonathan Stone, 'English Silver Rimmonim and their Makers' in *Quest 1*, 1965.

8. Ark curtain
   1923
   London
   Blue velvet, embroidered and appliquéd with metal threads, ribbons.
   H: 187cm, W: 183 cm
   Plymouth Hebrew Congregation

The community hung this curtain in front of the Ark in the synagogue. It is part of a set with a matching Torah mantle and Torah cover (not shown). The Torah cover has a maker's label which reads, "Specialists in tallisim & synagogue embroidery R. Mazin & Co. 144 Whitechapel Rd. London E.1". The curtain bears the inscription, "Donated by the women of Plymouth in the year 683 (= 1923)". This probably refers to a Ladies' Guild, which played an important role in almost every synagogue community.

9. Rimmonim
   Late seventeenth century
   Probably Dutch
   Silver, no marks
   H: 24 cm
   The Jewish Museum,
   London lent by
   Hampstead Synagogue

These Torah bells have small bulbous bodies, chased with acanthus foliage and with gilt flower finials. There are six pendant bells on long chains. One of the rimmonim is engraved, "These bells formerly the property of Falmouth Synagogue were acquired for the Hampstead Synagogue by Alexander Jacob". Such finials are the crowning glory of ritual silver and are used to adorn the wooden staves of the Torah.

Literature: A. Jacob, 'The Jews of Falmouth' in *The Transactions of The Jewish Historical Society of England 17*, 1951–2, pp. 71–2. Richard Barnett, *Catalogue of the Jewish Museum London*, cat. No. 104.

10. Decalogue
Early nineteenth century
Penzance
Wood painted dull green and gold
H: 76.2 cm, W: 64 cm
The Jewish Museum, London

This Decalogue (Ten Commandments) from the synagogue in Penzance has a double arcaded top supported on three turned columns. Together with an inscribed panel, it is all that remains of the interior furnishings of the synagogue, and its condition is such that it could not be displayed as it is now beyond restoration. The Hebrew is clearly the work of an amateur scribe. It has been painted over, possibly not by Jewish hands, and small errors have resulted.

11. Panel
    Early nineteenth century
    Penzance
    Wood, painted
    H: 14.5 cm, W: 127 cm
    Mr. and Mrs. Tony Gillman, Penzance

The panel and the Decalogue are all that is left of the Penzance Synagogue. Built in 1807–8, and eventually used as a place of worship by the Plymouth Brethren after 1906, the panel was still in place throughout this period until relatively recently. When the Brethren moved elsewhere, the building was sold to the Devenish Brewery. The translation of the Hebrew inscription reads, "Open to us the Gates of Mercy".

12. Torah Scroll
   Nineteenth century
   Parchment and wood
   L: 100 cm
   The Royal Institution of Cornwall, The
   Courtney Library, Truro

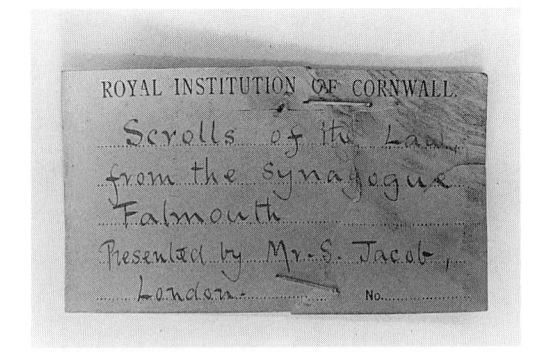

This large Torah Scroll, containing the Five Books of Moses, was presented to the Royal Institution of Cornwall by Mr. Samuel Jacob of London, formerly of Falmouth. This would have been some years after 1891 when the synagogue had been closed and Mr. Jacob had arranged for its repair and left for London. It is one of several scrolls which were deposited with The Royal Institution of Cornwall and whose whereabouts had been forgotten by the Jewish community.

13. Torah Binder
 1802
 Plymouth
 Natural fine cotton bound in yellow silk, embroidered and painted
 L: 292 cm, H: 15 cm
 The Susser Archive

A binder to wrap around the Torah was usually made from the diaper used at a boy's circumcision. It follows the continental Ashkenazi tradition (the family had emigrated from Bohemia) of preparing a binder for eventual use in the synagogue. To date, this is the only known extant one in Britain, where this charming custom was evidently not continued. This one reads, "Abraham ben Notta (Nathan) Katz born for good luck on Thursday 28 Kislev 5562 (=3/12/1802) May the Lord rear him to the Torah, to Chuppah (marriage) and to good deeds. Amen." In the centre is a painted Sagittarius, now very faded.

Literature: See Annette Weber, Evelyn Friedlander and Fritz Armbruster eds. *Mappot . . . blessed be who comes*, 1997, for a fuller explanation.

14. Torah Pointer
1815
Exeter
Silver, maker's mark SH (Simon Harris)
L: 30.5 cm
The Jewish Museum, London

The pointer, known in Hebrew as a *yad*, which means hand, has a spirally fluted shaft and an octagonal handle, divided by a basketwork knop with a matching finial. It is engraved with a Hebrew inscription which reads in translation, " Israel son of Naphtali Hirsch, Truro 5596 (=1836)". It was originally used in Falmouth Synagogue.

Literature: Richard Barnett, *Catalogue of the Jewish Museum London*, cat. No. 169.

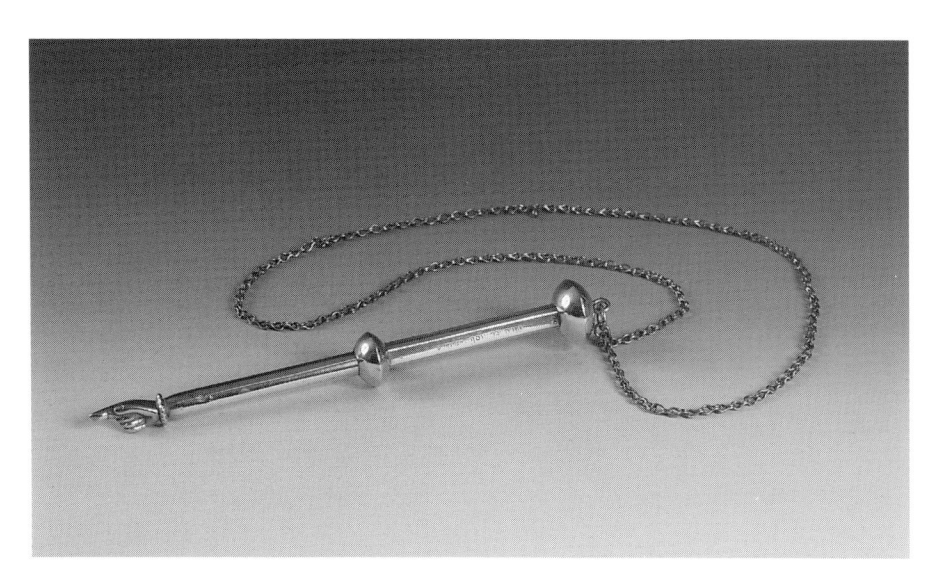

15. Torah Pointer
England
Early nineteenth century
Silver, no marks
L: 24.7 cm
The Jewish Museum, London

The pointer has a plain cylindrical shaft and handle with a compressed knop and finial. It is finished with a heavy chain. It is engraved in Hebrew with the names of four donors from Falmouth: Isaac b. Joseph, Yehuda b. Joseph, Isaac b. Joseph and Meyer b. Joseph.

Literature: Richard Barnett, *Catalogue of the Jewish Museum London*, cat. No. 170.

16. *Falmouth Harbour*
    William Flood
    1864
    Watercolour
    H: 20 cm, W: 28 cm
    Evelyn Friedlander, London

This painting by an unknown, possibly amateur artist, shows how little the view over the harbour at Falmouth has changed. He has taken some licence with the synagogue at the centre, and has turned it sideways, so that, from the artist's chosen angle, we see its long side. It was said that the Jewish merchants built the synagogue high on the hill, so that they could keep an eye on their ships entering and leaving the harbour.

17. Rimmonim
    1813
    Exeter
    Silver and parcel gilt, Exeter assay mark, maker's mark SH (Simon Harris)
    H: 38 cm
    Exeter Hebrew Congregation

These Torah finials consist of three open-work crowns in a tier, surmounted by a pineapple. The bells are inside the crowns. They bear the inscription, "Donated to the community of Exeter in the year 573 (=1813)". There is a certain similarity to two filigree pairs in the Sephardi synagogue in Amsterdam; the earlier of the latter dates back to 1728.

Literature: Bernard Susser, *The Jews of South-West England* 1993, p. 218. Jonathan Stone, 'English Silver Rimmonim and their Makers' in *Quest 1*, 1965, plate 14, p. 28.

18. Memorbook
    1857
    Exeter
    Manuscript
    H: 21 cm, W: 14 cm
    The Jewish Museum, London

The use of a memorial book is a very old custom, recalling the community's Ashkenazi antecedents. The earliest entry is for Reb Tevle Schiff, Rabbi of the Great Synagogue, London, the second for Reb Mordecai the martyr and the last entry is dated 2nd Teveth 1911. The first leaf is an ornamental title-page surmounted by trumpet-blowing cherubim. The front cover reads, "Book remembering the souls who went to their rest, who lived in the vicinity of Exeter and who have donated to charity. Written by Alexander b. Reb Eliezer in the year 'May their souls be bound up in the bundle of life'". The last phrase is a chronogram which gives the year, in this case 5618 (1857–8).

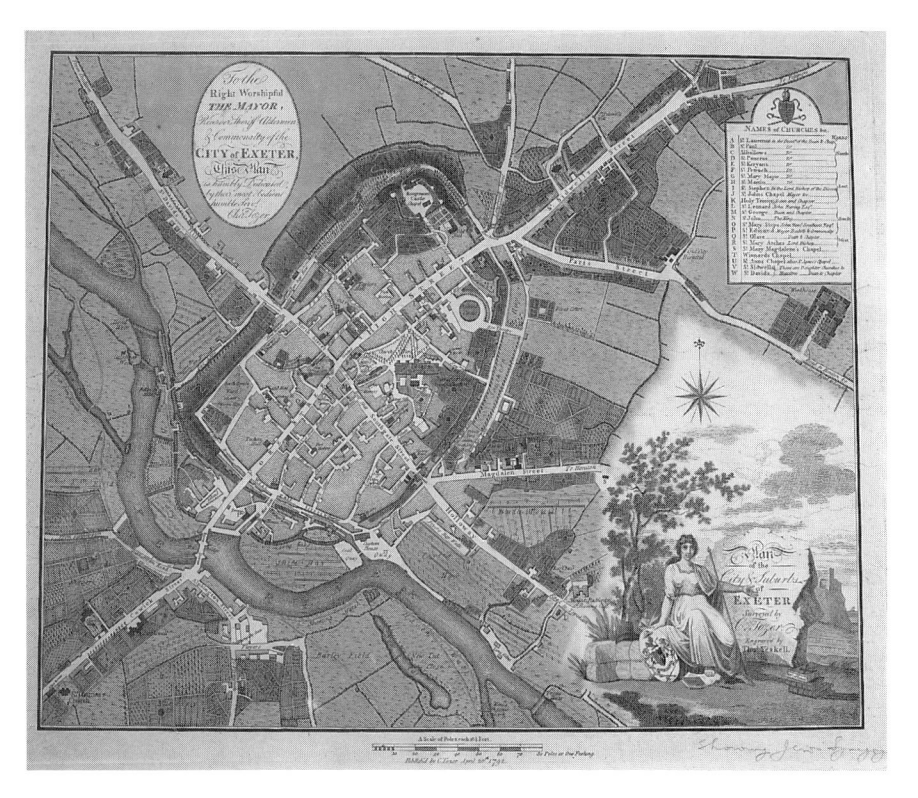

19. Exeter City Plan
   1792
   Exeter
   Print
   H: 37 cm, W: 45 cm
   The Jewish Museum, London

This plan of the City of Exeter was surveyed and published in 1792 by C. Tozer and engraved by T. Yeakell. In addition to a list of 23 city churches in the top right-hand corner, the synagogue of 1762 is marked between Fore Street and North Street.

20. Interior of Exeter Synagogue
    c.1910
    Exeter
    Photograph
    H: 24 cm, W: 19 cm
    Exeter Central Library

This photograph shows the synagogue early in the twentieth century, probably after the restoration paid for by descendants of the Rev. Sigmund Hoffnung, a former minister. The brass plaque on the right of the Ark, commemorating his ministry, is now lost. The Ark has been partially repainted with black and gold columns and urns, a dark green malachite-effect plinth, while the gallery columns have been stencilled in the style of Owen Jones. The building was lit by gas, vestiges of which remain. The wall panelling was lost in the 1960s but the recent restoration of the synagogue saw its return and the interior appears today much as it does in this photograph.

Frank Gent

21. Exterior of Exeter Synagogue
    c.1910
    Exeter
    Photograph
    H: 17 cm, W: 12 cm
    Exeter Central Library

In this photograph, the synagogue lies tucked into a narrow street, leading to working-class housing in the courts beyond. It faces a mattress factory. In contrast to these humble surroundings the synagogue façade looks splendid. This is the new façade of 1854, an imposing neo-classical structure of three storeys, which was lost, together with the building opposite, to bomb damage in the Second World War. The building to the right of the synagogue, formerly the caretaker's house and Hebrew school, was demolished for office redevelopment in the 1970s.

Frank Gent

22. *Exeter Synagogue Interior*
John White (1851–1933)
c.1900
Exeter
Photograph of watercolour
H: 31 cm, W: 21 cm
Royal Albert Memorial Museum, Exeter

This painting formed part of an album of eleven watercolours by various artists, commissioned by Sir Julian Goldsmid. White was born in Edinburgh and brought up in Australia, returning to Scotland in 1873. He studied at the Royal Scottish Academy, winning the Keith Prize in 1875. He exhibited widely and was elected to the Royal Institute of Painters in Watercolours in 1882. Later, he lived in the Devon village of Beer, where he was known as "Painter White". He is best known as a painter of landscape, marine and rustic genre pictures.

23. *Exeter Synagogue Exterior*
John White (1851–1933)
c.1900
Exeter
Photograph of watercolour
H: 31 cm, W: 21 cm
Royal Albert Memorial Museum, Exeter

This painting forms a pair with that of the Exeter synagogue interior, and also derives from the album commissioned by Sir Julian Goldsmid. It shows the 1854 façade of the synagogue which was lost as a result of bomb damage during the Second World War. Only the ground floor survived, and a new first floor was added in 1980.

89

24. Torah Shield
   1863–64
   Birmingham
   Silver, maker's mark GU (George Unité)
   H: 24 cm, W: 15.2 cm
   Exeter Hebrew Congregation

This shield or breastplate, used to decorate the Torah, is in the English style, with an open-work swagged bow and a heavy chain. It was donated in memory of Rosa, wife of Solomon son of Abraham Elsner, in the year 1864. She had died in 1861 and is buried in the Exeter Jewish Cemetery. Inside the front cover of the Exeter Memorbook, the name of S. Elsner, warden 5617 (= 1857) is inscribed.

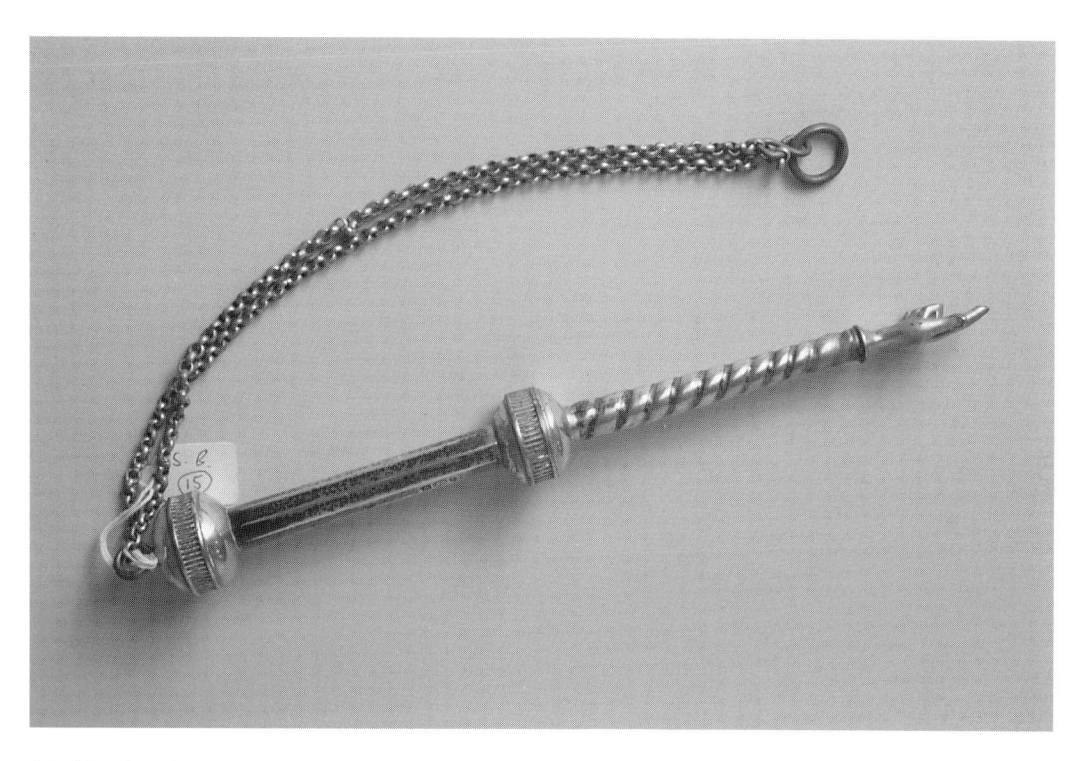

25. Torah Pointer
    1814
    Exeter
    Silver, maker's mark SH (Simon Harris of Plymouth Dock floruit 1811–1815)
    L: 29 cm
    Exeter Hebrew Congregation

The pointer has a barley twist shaft with an octagonal handle, divided by an incised knop with matching finial. It is engraved with a Hebrew inscription which records that it was the gift of Reb Shmuel son of Zvi Hart minister 574 (=1814). It is by the same maker as the Exeter Rimmonim dated 1813 (cat. no. 15) and the spoon (cat. no. 44).

Literature: Bernard Susser, *The Jews of South-West England*, 1993, p. 218.

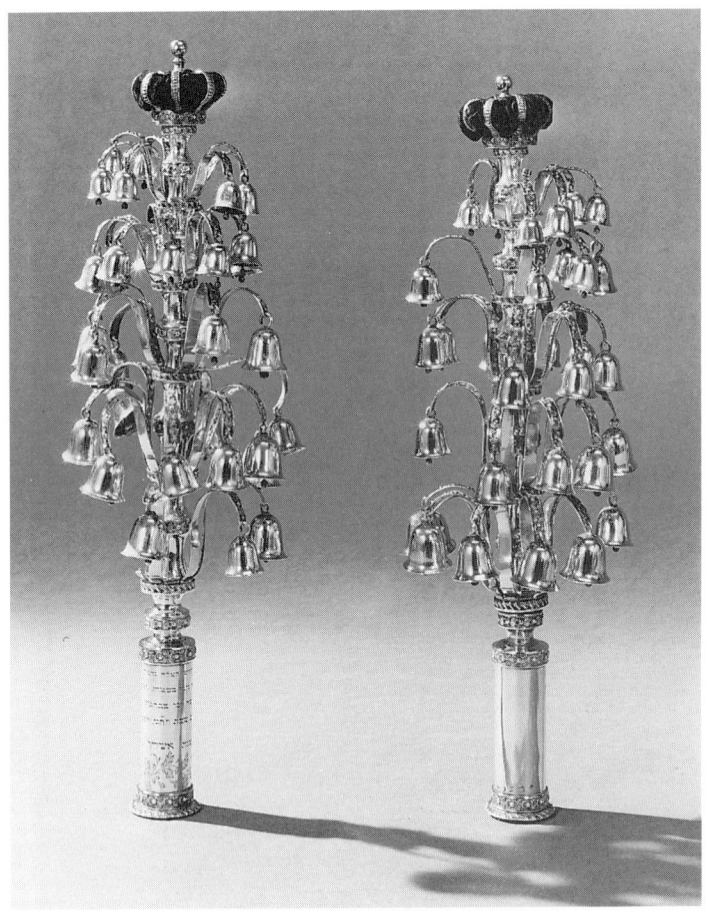

26. Rimmonim
    1811
    Exeter, maker's mark SL
    (Simon Levy)
    Silver and parcel gilt, velvet
    H: 42.5 cm
    Exeter Hebrew Congregation

These finials are of the bell-tree type, surmounted by a crown containing a velvet cushion (see catalogue no. 7). The base of one is inscribed, "Donated by the women and maidens of Exeter on Shabbat Chol haMoed 9th of Nissan"; the base of the other finial gives the names of the aforementioned seventeen ladies. They are by the same maker as the spoons (cat. no. 46).

Literature: Bernard Susser, *The Jews of South-West England* 1993, p. 218. (The date of the donation is incorrectly given here as 1821.) Jonathan Stone, 'English Silver Rimmonim and their Makers' in *Quest 1*, 1965, plate 16, p. 29.

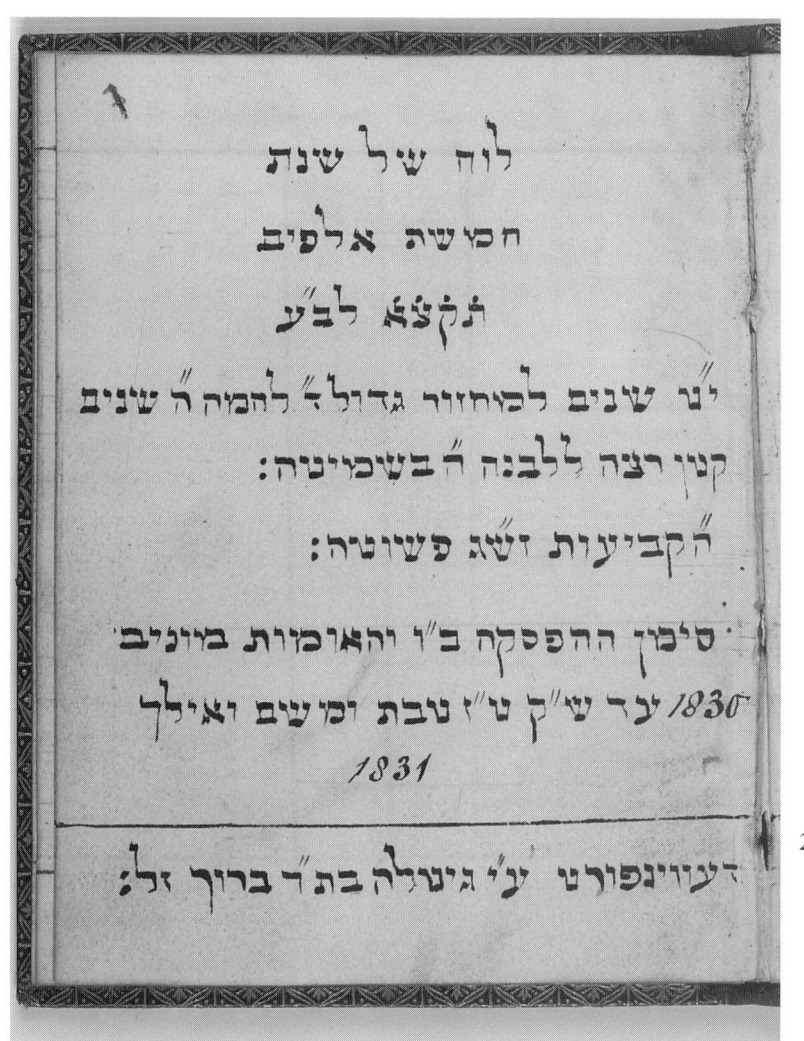

27. Calendar from
 Devonport
 1830/31
 Devonport
 Manuscript
 H: 11.5 cm, W: 9 cm
 The Jewish Museum,
 London

This calendar, in a style typical of the Ashkenazi domain, was written by Gittele bat Baruch of Devonport. It is not possible to tell whether she copied it from an extant calendar, many of which were published in Germany, or whether she was writing it to be printed in England. The cursive Hebrew handwriting is good, and she would have needed considerable knowledge to create the calendar from scratch.

28. Torah Mantle
    1902
    London?
    Blue velvet, metal thread, ribbon
    H: 79 cm
    Plymouth Hebrew Congregation

Such mantles are used to dress the Torah when it rests in the Ark. This example is of the round-top Sephardi type, with a fringe and a ribbon trim, embroidered with gold metal thread. In the centre is a depiction of the Decalogue (the Ten Commandments), surmounted by a Star of David and a crown, with the Hebrew initials of the words *Keter Torah*, the crown of the Torah. The Hebrew inscription reads in translation, "Donated by the Women's Society of Plymouth 1902".

29. Penzance Minute Book
1807–1829
Penzance
Manuscript
H: 19.5 cm,
W: 16 cm
From the Roth Collection,
Brotherton Library,
University of Leeds

This is the earliest of three minute-books to have survived from the Penzance Jewish community and they cover (with gaps) the years 1807–1892. They shed light on the running of the synagogue, record gifts of ritual objects and synagogue furnishings, and reflect contemporary attitudes towards their ministers and to charity. There is an inventory of synagogue property and a list of regulations. The language used is sometimes a mixture of Judeo-German, Hebrew and English.

30. Lemon Hart Rum Bottle
Glass, rum
H: 28.5 cm
Dr. Helen Fry

Once, this was one of the best known of all brands of rum, although latterly few have realised that it was named for a Jew called Lemon Hart from Penzance. Originally a pure Jamaican rum, it is now blended with rums from Barbados, Guyana and Trinidad. Lemon Hart's company, started by his grandfather in the early eighteenth century, was continued by his only son David, trading as Lemon Hart & Son. Morris and Gilbey bought the firm in 1879 and it eventually became a part of United Rum Merchants Ltd., and today is in the portfolio of Allied Domecq.

31. *Lemon Hart*
    c.1820
    Painter unknown
    Oil on canvas
    H: 126 cm, W: 100 cm, framed
    Rev. Canon and Mrs R. Stranack,
    Bude

Lemon Hart (1768–1845) was born in Penzance, where he lived and worked until he moved to London early in the nineteenth century. He took over his grandfather's wine and spirit business and made it renowned, but he was also an active and committed member of the Penzance community, even from afar. He presented the synagogue with various ritual objects at different times, was charitable, and was even instrumental in the hiring of Barnett Simmons as a minister in 1811.

32. *Mary Hart* (née Solomon)
c.1820
Painter unknown
Oil on canvas
H: 126 cm, W: 100 cm, framed
Rev. Canon and Mrs R. Stranack, Bude

Mary Solomon was Lemon Hart's second wife, his first having died tragically in a fire in 1803, and they had no children. Mary died in 1852 and is buried in the same cemetery as her husband in Brady Street, London. Both this painting and the one of Lemon Hart are in the possession of descendants of his family.

33. *Exeter Cathedral*
　 Solomon A. Hart RA
　 (1806–1881)
　 Watercolour
　 1833
　 H: 24 cm,
　 W: 16.5 cm
　 Ben Uri Art Society
　 London

34. *Self-Portrait*
   Solomon A. Hart RA (1806–1881)
   Oil on canvas
   H: 60 cm, W: 48 cm
   Royal Albert Memorial Museum, Exeter

Solomon Alexander Hart was the first Jew to be admitted to the Royal Academy in 1840, and in 1864 was appointed its librarian, a post he occupied with distinction until his death. He was born in Plymouth, and throughout his life remained deeply attached to his native city. He painted many historical pictures, and numerous portraits of prominent members of the Jewish community.

Exhibited: Belgrave Gallery 1978

35. *Henry Ezekiel*
Abraham Solomon
1845
Graphite and pastel (photograph)
H: 45 cm, W: 34.2 cm
The Jewish Museum, London

Henry Ezekiel (1772–1835) was the brother of the better-known and more talented Ezekiel Ezekiel. He, too, was an engraver, silversmith, watchmaker and optician in Exeter. After Ezekiel Ezekiel's relatively early death, at the age of 49, Henry and his sisters carried on the business, and though he may have lacked his brother's artistic genius, he was more successful financially. The Jewish Museum also has on display a fine portrait in oil of Henry painted by Abraham Solomon.

36. *Betsy Ezekiel*
Abraham Solomon
1845
Graphite and pastel
(photograph)
H: 46.5 cm,
W: 36 cm
The Jewish Museum, London

Betsy was the daughter of the minister of the Exeter Synagogue, Moses Horwitz Levy, and it was there that she married Henry on 14th March 1810 at the age of 28. She appears to have brought with her a very considerable fortune. They had three daughters. This pastel shows her in prosperous middle age.

37. Medal
   Ezekiel A. Ezekiel
   1790
   Exeter
   Silver, engraved
   Diam. 5.5 cm
   Topsham Museum

Ezekiel A. Ezekiel (1757–1806) had only very few items hall-marked at the Exeter Assay Office. There were eight silver medals and a seal, of which this is the only medal to have survived. It was presented to William Morrish, aged 12 years, for penmanship on 18th June 1790. He was a pupil at Palmer's Boarding School, Topsham.

Frank Gent

38. Banknote
   Ezekiel A. Ezekiel
   1804
   Paper
   H: 10 cm,
   W: 18 cm
   Archive Service, Lloyds Bank TSB Group

As part of his work as an engraver, Ezekiel produced this banknote design for Barings Bank of Exeter. There were numerous small banks producing their own banknotes throughout the provinces at that time, many of which failed. This note should be compared with a modern one to appreciate the skill of Ezekiel's penmanship. He combines blackletter and copperplate with attractive flourishes. The note is signed below the left-hand cartouche.

Frank Gent

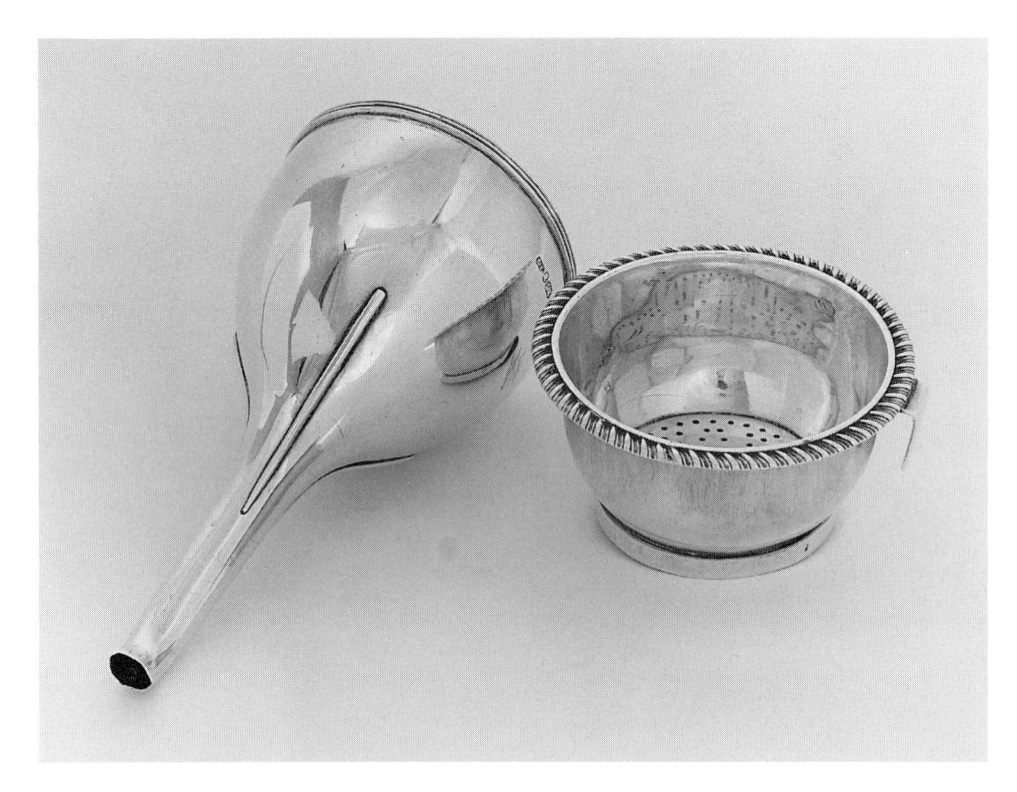

39. Wine Strainer
   Simon Levy
   1823
   Exeter
   Silver
   L: 16.2 cm, Diam: 8 cm
   Royal Albert Memorial Museum, Exeter

The funnel is plain with a reeded border of parallel lines. There is a separate strainer with a gadrooned edge and hook. Gadrooning is a heavily lobed decoration typical of late eighteenth-century and Regency silver. The funnel was used for decanting wine to remove any sediment, and is typical of the fine quality goods made for wealthier clients of this period. (See also cat. nos. 26 and 46.)

Frank Gent

40. Naval Jacket
    c.1810
    Wool and gilt
    H: 101.5 cm, W: 68.5 cm
    The Museum of North Devon, Barnstaple:
    accession no. 1991.813

This jacket was worn by Dr Simon Gage Britton of Bristol and Barnstaple. He qualified as first assistant surgeon at St. Bartholomew's Hospital in 1803, and joined the Navy later that year. Qualifying as a surgeon in 1805, he transferred to *The Victory* during the Battle of Trafalgar. He is believed to be depicted in A.W. Davis's celebrated painting of the death of Nelson. In this period, many Jews were slopmen or slopsellers, slops being ready-made clothing worn by seamen, which ultimately evolved into a uniform. Thus, this jacket may well have been made by Jews.

Alison Mills

41. *Jacob Solomon*
   Artist unknown
   Mid-nineteenth century
   Oil on canvas
   H: 69 cm, W: 59 cm
   The Jewish Museum, London

Jacob Solomon (1782–1857) was born in Europe. His father was from Lissa in Poland, and according to family tradition, was the *chazan* (cantor) and *shochet* (slaughterer) of the Exeter synagogue, as the congregation was too poor to afford a full-time rabbi. Initially a jeweller, by 1830 he listed himself as a quill dresser and cutter. In that year, the family migrated to London by sailing ship, and he established a wholesale hardware business at 60 Tothill Street, Westminster. He traded with Exeter, Plymouth and Portsmouth in quills, cutlery, clocks, watches, brass and silverware.

Edgar Samuel

42. *Mrs. Jacob Solomon*
    Artist unknown
    Mid-nineteenth century
    Oil on canvas
    H: 69 cm, W: 59 cm
    The Jewish Museum, London

Sarah Solomon née Phillips (1789–1875) was born in Plymouth where, according to family tradition, her father was a *shochet* (ritual slaughterer). She and her husband had twelve children and numerous descendants.

Edgar Samuel

43. Moss J. Jacob
   Mid-nineteenth century
   Falmouth
   Photograph of painting
   H: 27 cm, W: 21 cm
   Alex Jacob Archive

Moses (or Moss) Jacob Jacob (1812–1860) was a native of Falmouth, and a descendant, probably his great-grandson, of the first Jew known to have settled there around 1740, Alexander Moses, known as Zender Falmouth. From his trade card as well as his photograph, it is reasonable to assume that he achieved a fair degree of prosperity.

44. Mrs. Moss J. Jacob
Mid-nineteenth century
Falmouth
Photograph of painting
H: 26 cm, W: 20 cm
Alex Jacob Archive

Frances Jacob née Emanuel (1812–1875) came from Portsea.

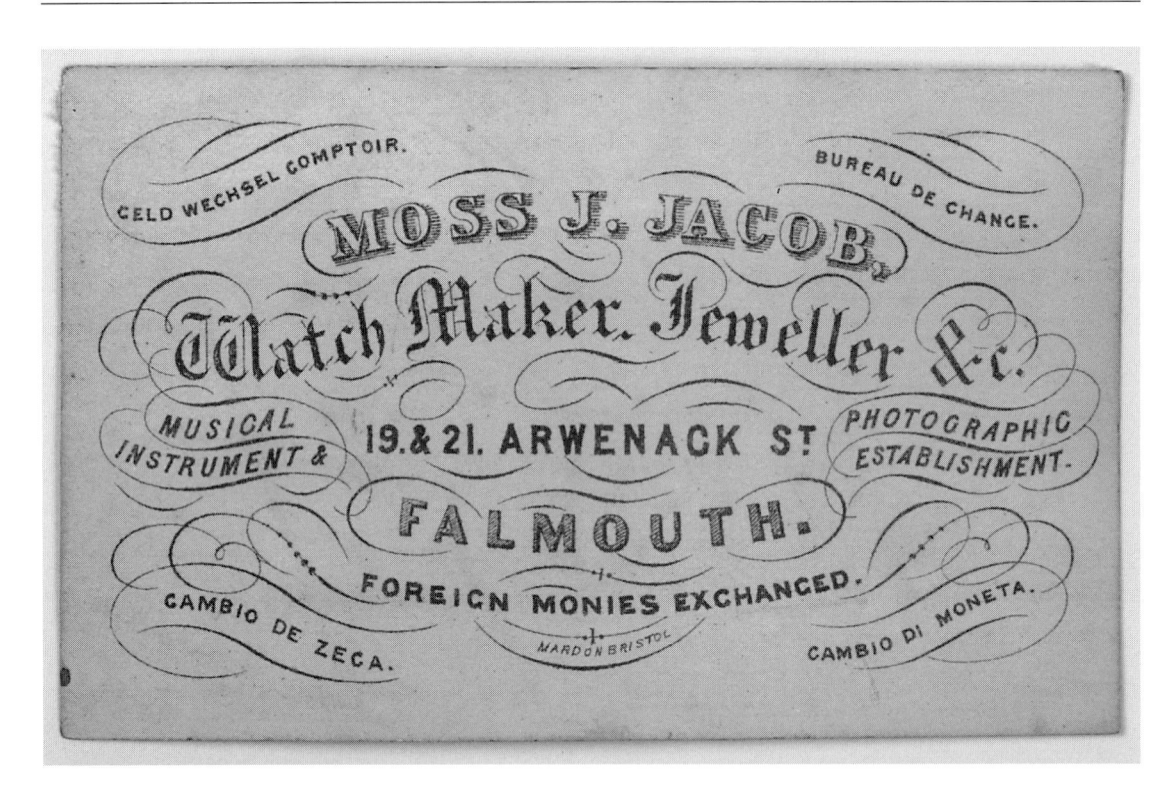

45. Trade Card
Mid-nineteenth century
Card
H: 4.5 cm, W: 7.5 cm
The Jewish Museum, London

This finely engraved trade card by Mardon of Bristol is typical of the period and also indicates the wide range of services offered by one emporium, that of Moss J. Jacob. He advertises himself as a watchmaker and jeweller, whose shop is a photographic establishment also dealing in musical instruments, as well as offering the exchange of foreign monies, in various languages. Most of these are areas of trade with which many Jews were associated at that time.

46. Five Dessert Spoons
   Simon Levy
   1828
   Exeter
   Silver, hallmark m
   L: 18 cm, bowl L: 6.1 cm,
   W: 3.8 cm
   Frank Gent

Simon Levy, like his father Emanuel, produced large quantities of domestic silver that was assayed at Exeter Assay Office. In October 1818, for example, he had hall-marked 17 dozen teaspoons, 42 salt spoons, 14 dessert spoons, 4 mustard spoons, 4 butter knives, 12 forks, 2 sugar tongs, 1 jug, 1 coffee pot, 6 teapots and 2 "nossels" (nozzles? or possibly candle-holders). These were sold to local families, often gentry, and frequently engraved with a family crest, as with these dessert spoons. His work is typical of the period, and of good quality workmanship.

Frank Gent

47. Spoon
   Simon Harris
   1813
   Plymouth Dock
   Silver, hallmark R
   L: 26.6 cm, bowl L: 8 cm,
   W: 4.9 cm
   Frank Gent

Large table or serving spoon by Simon Harris, who was active from 1811–1815. It is engraved with the initials JMM.

48. *Barnett A. Simmons*
R.T. Pentreath
c.1839
Penzance
Oil on canvas
H: 81 cm,
W: 71 cm
Penlee House Art
Gallery and Museum
(long-term loan from
the Simmons family)

Barnett Asher Simmons (1784–1860) was the longest-serving minister to the Jewish community of Penzance, arriving there in December 1811, and remaining, with breaks, until 1859. He also served the congregation as its *mohel* (circumcisor) and *shochet* (ritual slaughterer). He retired in 1854, and, together with his wife, went to live with a married daughter in Merthyr Tydfil. Three years later, they returned and he served the congregation for two final years. He is buried in the Jewish cemetery in Penzance.

49. *Mrs. Barnett A. Simmons*
R.T. Pentreath
c.1839
Penzance
Oil on canvas
H: 81 cm, W: 71 cm
Penlee House Art Gallery and Museum (long-term loan from the Simmons family)

Flora Simmons née Jacob (1790–1874) was the daughter of Moses Jacob of Falmouth, and the grand-daughter of Alexander Moses, who was known as Zender Falmouth. She herself was born in Redruth, and bore her husband 11 children. After her husband's death, she returned to Merthyr Tydfil where she died. She is buried in the Jewish cemetery there.

50. Alderman Myer Fredman JP
    1911
    Devonport
    Photograph
    H: 40 cm, W: 30 cm
    Mrs. Jack Clarfelt, London

Scion of a distinguished Plymouth family, he became Mayor of Devonport in 1911, the first Jew to be so honoured. He served on the Devonport council for 34 years until his death in 1927. Undoubtedly, he would have gone on to become the first Jewish Mayor of Plymouth, had he not died relatively young. As it was, this honour was conferred on Arthur Goldberg in 1961.

51. Mrs. Myer Fredman
    c.1911
    Devonport
    Photograph
    H: 40 cm, W: 30 cm
    Mrs. Jack Clarfelt, London

Rebecca Fredman was the much-loved wife of Myer and predeceased him. Many years later, a pair of stained-glass windows in the *succah* (tabernacle) of the synagogue in Plymouth were donated by their children in their memory.

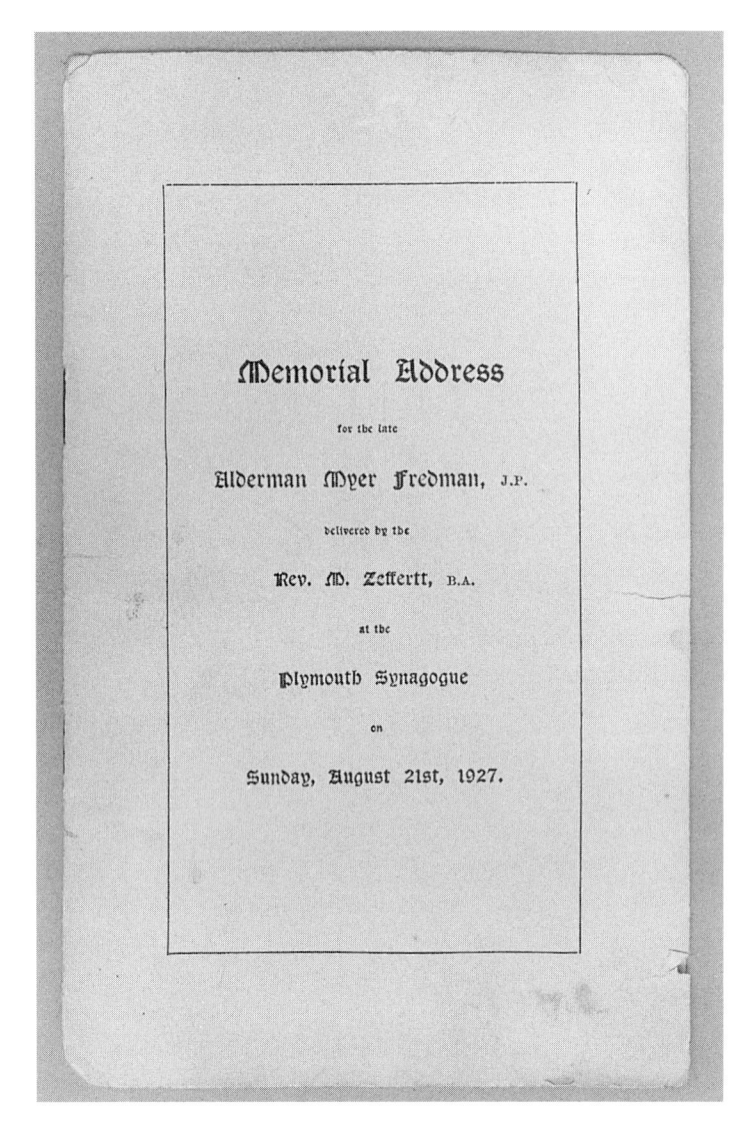

> **Memorial Address**
>
> for the late
>
> Alderman Myer Fredman, J.P.
>
> delivered by the
>
> Rev. M. Zeffertt, B.A.
>
> at the
>
> Plymouth Synagogue
>
> on
>
> Sunday, August 21st, 1927.

52. Myer Fredman Memorial
    Service Address
    1927
    Plymouth
    Paper
    H: 21.5 cm, W: 13.5 cm
    Mrs. Jack Clarfelt, London

The address at Myer Fredman's Memorial Service was delivered by the Rev. M. Zeffert on 21st August 1927. From it can be ascertained that not only was Fredman a devoted servant of his native city, but also a devout Jew, much attached to his synagogue. It had become possible for a Jew to live a life of commitment to the wider community, without in any way having to sacrifice his or her Jewish identity.

Glossary

Ashkenazim German Jews and their descendants in eastern and central Europe.

Bar (or bat) Mitzvah 'Son (or daughter) of the Commandment'. As a 13 year-old, a child is initiated into the adult Jewish community, and required to keep the precepts of the Torah.

Bimah Reading desk or pulpit.

B'rit Milah Circumcision, sign of the covenant between God and Israel.

Cantor The man who leads the synagogue service, chanting the prayers.

Challah Braided bread used in Sabbath evening home celebrations.

Cheder Religion school.

Chevra Kaddisha Charitable society with special responsibility for the sick and the dying, and for preparing the dead for burial and caring for their dependants.

Chuppah Wedding canopy. Also used as a term for marriage.

Diaspora 'Dispersal', a term for the Jewish people in exile outside biblical Palestine.

Kaddish Prayer for the dead.

Kashrut The dietary laws.

Kiddush Blessing over wine in the Sabbath and festivals.

Kosher 'Fit or suitable' food that an observant Jew may eat.

Mappa or *wimpel*. Torah binder.

Megillah Scroll of Esther.

Menorah Seven-branched candlestick.

Mikveh Gathering of living water i.e. spring or rainwater, which was prescribed for immersion for ritual cleaning purposes.

Minyan Quorum of ten men required as a minimum for Orthodox prayer.

GLOSSARY

Mohel 'Circumcisor', specially trained person who carries out the ceremony of circumcision.

Ohel 'Tent', chapel for prayers at the cemetery.

Parnas President of the synagogue.

Rabbi 'Teacher', appointed by the community and responsible for the interpretation and supervision of the texts and religious laws. In the Middle Ages, these fields were under the jurisdiction of rabbis to a very great degree. In modern times, rabbis have taken on much more of a pastoral function.

Reb An honorific title.

Rimmonim 'Pomegranates', the finials or bells which crown the staves of the Torah Scroll, usually of silver.

Rosh Hashanah The Jewish New Year.

Sephardim Jews of Spanish or Portuguese descent.

Shammas The beadle of a synagogue.

Shema The central prayer of Judaism.

Shochet Ritual slaughterer.

Shool, Shul 'School', designates the synagogue.

S'michah Rabbinic ordination.

Succah 'Tabernacle', used on the festival of Tabernacles.

Talmud A commentary and compendium of rabbinic laws.

Torah The Pentateuch, the Five Books of Moses. Also used to designate the teachings of the religious laws.

Torani Hebrew scholar.

Yad 'Hand', Torah pointer.

Selected Bibliography

Richard Barnett, *Catalogue of the Jewish Museum London*, 1974
G. L. Green, *The Royal Navy and Anglo-Jewry, 1740–1820*, 1989
A. G. Grimwade et al. (eds.) *Treasures of a London Temple*, London, 1951
Bernard Susser, *The Jews of South-West England*, Exeter 1993
S. A. Hart, *Reminiscences*, 1882
Edward Jamilly, *The Georgian Synagogue*, London 1999
Sharman Kadish, *Building Jerusalem*, London 1996
Keith Pearce and Helen Fry (eds.), *The Lost Jews of Cornwall*, Bristol 2000
Cecil Roth, *A History of the Jews of England*, (3rd edition) Oxford, 1964
Cecil Roth, *The Rise of Provincial Jewry*, London, 1950
Kathryn Salomon, *Jewish Ceremonial Embroidery*, London, 1988
Jonathan Stone, 'English Silver Rimmonim and their Makers' in *Quest 1*, 1965
Annette Weber, Evelyn Friedlander, Fritz Armbruster (eds.), *Mappot . . . blessed be who comes*, Osnabrück, 1997

Contributors

Fritz Armbruster is the designer of the Haus der Bayerischen Geschichte, Augsburg, Germany. He also works as an artist.

Evelyn Friedlander is the Director of The Hidden Legacy Foundation, London.

Rabbi Albert H. Friedlander is the emeritus Rabbi of Westminster Synagogue and Dean of Leo Baeck College.

Dr. Helen Fry is a Consultant and Research Fellow at University College, London.

Frank Gent is the Education Officer at the Royal Albert Memorial Museum, Exeter.

Rabbi Frank Dabba Smith is the Rabbi of Harrow and Wembley Progressive Synagogue and a photographer.

Julia Weiner is the Education Officer at the Courtauld Institute.

Acknowledgements

Thanks are due to the following:

Victor Bishop, Norwich
Elizabeth Brock, Penzance
Angela Broome, Courtney Library, Truro
Tamsin Daniel, The Royal Cornwall Museum, Truro
Eric Dawkins, Falmouth
Margaret Dobie, London
Rabbi Dr. Albert Friedlander, Leo Baeck College, London
Dr. Martin Fry, University College, London
Bennie Greenberg, Plymouth Hebrew Congregation
Thena Heshel, Totnes
Jonathan Holmes, Penzance
Alisa Jaffa, The Jewish Museum, London
Edward Jamilly, London
Martina Krüger, Textile Conservation Centre, Winchester
Emil Künzel
Sevim and Ali Ledin
Ian Lillicrapp, London
Jennifer Marin, The Jewish Museum, London
Alison Mills, Museum of North Devon, Barnstaple
Keith Pearce, Penzance
Camilla Previté, Sotheby's
Edgar Samuel, London
Michael Shapiro, London
Godfrey Simmons, Bromsgrove
Rabbi Mark Solomon, Leo Baeck College
Dr. Hermann Süß, Rostock University Library
Hanna Susser, Jerusalem
Mika Takami, Textile Conservation Centre, Winchester
Cedric Tarsky, Plymouth Hebrew Congregation
The Textile Conservation Centre, Winchester
Charles Tucker, London
Victor Tunkel, London
Dr. Annette Weber, Jewish Museum, Frankfurt
Caroline Worthington, Royal Albert Memorial Museum, Exeter

Photo credits

By catalogue number:

1. Royal Cornwall Museum, Truro
2. no credit
3. Frank Dabba Smith
4. Frank Dabba Smith
5. Susser Archive
6. Frank Dabba Smith
7. Frank Dabba Smith
8. Frank Dabba Smith
9. Ian Lillicrapp, The Jewish Museum, London
10. Ian Lillicrapp, The Jewish Museum, London
11. Frank Dabba Smith
12. Frank Dabba Smith
13. Frank Dabba Smith
14. Ian Lillicrapp, The Jewish Museum, London
15. Ian Lillicrapp, The Jewish Museum, London
16. Frank Dabba Smith
17. Frank Dabba Smith
18. Ian Lillicrapp, The Jewish Museum, London
19. Ian Lillicrapp, The Jewish Museum, London
20. Devon Library and Information Services
21. Devon Library and Information Services
22. Royal Albert Memorial Museum, Exeter
23. Royal Albert Memorial Museum, Exeter
24. Frank Dabba Smith
25. Frank Dabba Smith
26. Susser Archive
27. Ian Lillicrapp, The Jewish Museum, London
28. Frank Dabba Smith
29. Brotherton Library, Leeds
30. Frank Dabba Smith
31. Focus Photography, Bradninch

PHOTO CREDITS

32. Focus Photography, Bradninch
33. Ben Uri Art Society, London
34. Royal Albert Memorial Museum, Exeter
35. Ian Lillicrapp, The Jewish Museum, London
36. Ian Lillicrapp, The Jewish Museum, London
37. Royal Albert Memorial Museum, Exeter
38. Leo Maggs
39. Royal Albert Memorial Museum, Exeter
40. Frank Dabba Smith
41. Ian Lillicrapp, The Jewish Museum, London
42. Ian Lillicrapp, The Jewish Museum, London
43. Alex Jacob Archive
44. Alex Jacob Archive
45. Ian Lillicrapp, The Jewish Museum, London
46. Frank Gent, Exeter
47. Frank Gent, Exeter
48. Penlee House Art Gallery and Museum
49. Penlee House Art Gallery and Museum
50. Frank Dabba Smith
51. Frank Dabba Smith
52. Frank Dabba Smith

و